ROBERT COX

IF ONLY I COULD READ

ROBERT COX

KEITHWALKERBOOKS, INC
This is a UMS production

IF ONLY I COULD READ

KEITHWALKERBOOKS

Publishing Company
KeithWalkerBooks, Inc.
P.O. Box 690
Allen, TX 75013

All rights reserved. Except for use in any review, the reproduction or utilization of this manuscript in whole or partial in any form by any mechanical, electronic, or other means, not known or hereafter invented, including photocopying, xerography, and recording, or in any information retrieval or storage system, is forbidden without written permission of the publisher, KeithWalkerBooks, Inc.

For information write
KeithWalkerBooks, Inc.
P.O. Box 690
Allen, TX 75013

All characters in this book have no existence outside the imagination of the author and have no relation whatsoever to anyone bearing the same name or names. They are not even distantly inspired by any individual known or unknown to the author and all incidents are pure invention.

ISBN-13 DIGIT: 978-1-7320624-6-7
ISBN-10 DIGIT: 1732062463

Manufactured in the United States of America

Visit us at www.keithwalkerbooks.com

ACKNOWLEGEMENTS

I would first like to thank God for his everlasting love and compassion. I could not have accomplished anything in life, if not for His grace and mercy. This book would not have been possible without my beautiful wife, Pat. I'm grateful for her strong encouragement and help with revising and editing. I would also like to thank Larry Williams, PhD, for his encouragement to include the tragedy with the small boy. Special thanks to Esther Stoker, reading specialist and playwright, my brothers David and Sherrill, Dan Bryant, a good friend, neighbor, and professional photographer, and Keith Thomas Walker, author and editor, for his outstanding guidance.

FORWARD

As a writer, editor, and small-time publisher, I'm often approached by writers who need advice on a book they're working on. My passion for the craft has led me to always keep an open mind and receive those seeking my assistance with an attentive ear. I'm so glad I maintained this level of compassion when I was contacted by Mr. Cox.

I must say, I've never met anyone quite like Robert. Many of my contacts have a story to tell, but you'd be hard pressed to find someone who has lived a more colorful and inspiring life.

When Robert told me that he spent the majority of his life unable to read and was unable to figure out why he couldn't read, I was immediately intrigued. As an English teacher, teaching students to read well, understand what they've read and pour out their thoughts with stimulating sentences is what I do best. The thought of making it all the way to the age of 50 without being able to do any of this, for me, is as baffling as it is compelling. I was instantly hooked on the plot of Robert's book.

As I read the rough draft, it became obvious that Robert's unadorned style of storytelling was deceiving. His writing gave birth to a tale of a man who, try as he might, could not master a fundamental human need. I was engrossed in his trials and tribulations, his successes and his failures. I was amazed that he had managed to live a life filled with more accolades than the average man could accumulate in three lifetimes – all without the ability to read.

I would obviously recommend this book to anyone who has faced similar challenges, but it would be wrong to limit this book to a particular audience. Any reader would benefit from this unique and well-told autobiography.

I know Robert believes the time and energy I've put into this project is a blessing. I hope he understands the feeling is completely mutual.

Keith Thomas Walker

IF ONLY I COULD READ

CHAPTER 1

I remember turning six. All I knew was that I would be starting school in September. I was so excited and also very scared. Because it was, for me, the unknown. My brother David, who was two years younger, would tell me that he was going to school too. I would get so mad, even after I started to school. When I would come home in the afternoons, David would tell me, just to get me angry, that he had gone to school too. It worked and I got plenty angry.

I do remember, in first grade, the first book we started to read. It was titled *"Dick, Jane, and Spot"*. I recall reading that book to my mother with no problem.

My brothers Sherrill and David and myself (l-r)

At that time there was a very tragic event that happened in my life. It was too much for any six-year-old boy to handle.

I hesitated for many months about putting this tragic event into print. I have discussed this with family members, family counselors, and a playwright. All have told me that this event needs to be in this book to illustrate the difficulties that I, and perhaps, others, have had in life.

The event occurred when I was in the first grade. One day I was playing, along with some other boys, at a friend's house. We were all inside the house when my friend came into the room with a pistol that belonged to his father. I remember someone taking the bullets out of the pistol. We all passed it around, admiring the look of the gun, the weight, and the shine. The next thing I remember, I had the gun in my hand. My friend's little brother was in the room sitting on the floor across from me. I did not know that the bullets had been put back into the pistol. I pulled the trigger. The blast of the gun was like thunder in the small room, scaring me to death. I looked around in confusion and realized the bullet had struck the little boy sitting on the floor across from me and killed him.

Frantically, I did what any horrified child would do. I jumped to my feet and ran. I had no idea where I was going. My only thought was to flee my horrible mistake. Sometime later in the afternoon, I found myself hiding in a very large doghouse in the yard across the street from my house. I will never forget the smell of the earth and the scent of the dog that once lived there. I could hear people calling my name, but I was too afraid to show myself. Fear and shame overwhelmed me. A policeman came by the doghouse, looked in and saw me. He told me to come out and reached in and grabbed me by the hand.

To this day, I do not remember leaving my friend's house, finding a doghouse three blocks away, or getting back home. Almost everything about that day, and several years later, is a blank. My mother took me out of the school I went to and enrolled me in another. I didn't understand at the time, but she was trying to protect me.

Until my junior year in high school, I was successful in going on with my life as if that tragedy had never happened.

I have been told by counselors that I have suffered from post-traumatic stress disorder. For my own sanity, I hope the memories of that tragic day never return to me. I have prayed many times that the family of that little boy has forgiven me.

In my first-grade year, I was very sick with chickenpox, then the measles and the mumps. Back in the early 40s, a household with someone diagnosed with a contagious disease was quarantined. This meant that until everyone had been cleared, the entire household was isolated. I missed so much school during this time, I did not have the number of days required to pass to the second grade. So, I repeated the first grade. In second grade, I fell sick again, and I spent a significant amount of time in various hospitals, including Scottish Rite Hospital for Children, Medical Arts, and Baylor Hospital.

At one point, the doctors told my parents that they would have to move to Arizona because the drier climate would be healthier for me. Miracles of miracles, at Baylor Hospital, the physicians found a small splinter of wood in the right lower lobe of my lung. Instead of the lung deteriorating the wood, as would have been expected, the wood deteriorated my lung. By then, I was a year and a half behind in school.

When I finally returned to school, I found myself with a problem that would haunt me for decades. Reading. I could not make sense of the words and letters in the books our teacher gave us, and I could not imagine what was wrong with me. The rest of the students seemed to be doing just fine. I began to feel stupid, and I did not know what to do about it. I didn't dare tell anyone about the problems I was having. I was so embarrassed.

At the age of seven, another aspect of my life was troubling. My mother and stepfather owned several bars, which we called "beer joints" at the time.

While my mother and stepfather worked in the evenings at the bars, they would take me and my two younger brothers to the movie theatre on Elm Street in downtown Dallas. I was responsible for taking care of my two brothers David and Sherrill, while my parents worked. David was two years younger, and Sherrill was a year and a half younger than David.

We loved to watch Westerns, Hop-Along Cassidy, Gene Autry, Roy Rogers, and Tarzan. Sometimes we'd see movies about Frankenstein, which really scared Sherrill. I'd find him hiding under the theatre seat or running out of the theatre. When he did that, David and I were tasked with finding him. I still recall him running through the aisles and in front of other people. Phew, that's was lot of responsibility for young children!

Often it was late when the movie let out. Everything else in downtown Dallas was closed. We'd sit on the curb in front of the theatre and wait for my mother or stepfather, Virgil. After they picked us up, they'd take us back to the bar. My brothers and I had to wait in the car until closing time. My parents would check on us. They'd bring us hamburgers and Grapettes to eat and drink in the car.

The beer joints created another unsettling problem. There were times that I'd wake up in the morning and find a strange man in bed with me. I guess he was too drunk to drive home the night before or had no place to go.

I did not like this way of living at all.

At Christmas time, our parents bought us each a set of cap guns and air rifle BB guns. At that time, it was common for boys to play cowboys and Indians.

One night, sometime after Christmas, my parents were back to their usual routine at the beer joints. As was their custom, they dropped us off at the movie theatre downtown, while they were at the bar. We got out late and went back to the bar until closing time. On this night, I was still awake when my stepfather Virgil return to the car.

There were several people following him, including my mother. It was obvious that there was a problem. One of the men in the group backed my stepfather against the car door. They were arguing about something. My eyes grew wide with fright. I was scared this man was going to hurt Virgil.

Without much forethought about my actions or the consequences, I rolled the window down, got my new BB gun, stuck it out the window and shot the man right in the face. I told my brother David to get his gun. All of the people standing around outside, including my mother, scattered back into the bar.

My stepfather got into the car. He turned and looked at me. He didn't say a word as he started driving us home. When we were almost there, he turned to me again and said, "Why did you do that?"

I told him that I thought the man was going to hurt him. I knew that, by morning, I would be in a lot of trouble. To my surprise, no one said another word about it, and I was so glad.

I must say that my stepfather was a very good person. He was good to me and to my brothers. He even read comic books to us.

School continued to be a nightmare for me. I continued to struggle with reading, and now math became a problem. It seemed to me that the other kids in my class were having fun and enjoying school. I was envious of them. I remember asking myself, "What is wrong with me?" Why am I so stupid and dumb that I cannot *get it*?

When I was around eight years old, Mom, David, Sherrill, and I, moved to Davis Street in Oak Cliff. At that time, she owned a different beer joint, and we lived in the back of this one. There was a 3-foot wall that enclosed the patio in the front. My brothers and I would play there, running back and forth over the wall, playing cowboys and Indians. It was fun shooting our cap guns at each other.

Mother enrolled me a new school, which was only three blocks away from our home. It was close enough for me to walk home during lunch. One day one of the teacher's saw me leaving the school grounds. She stopped me and told me that I wasn't allowed to leave and had to eat lunch at school. That evening I told my mother. She got very angry and went up to the school the next day to complain. That did no good. I was upset that I couldn't go home for lunch anymore. To top it all off, my grades were terrible. I had no idea what was wrong with me.

At that time, there were streetcars that ran up and down Jefferson Avenue and into downtown Dallas. Mother would let us walk up to Jefferson, catch the streetcar and ride downtown to see a movie. The streetcar had to cross Trinity River to get there. Because it rocked back and forth over the river, we were absolutely terrified. After the movie, we rode the streetcar back to Oak Cliff. Then we'd walk the six to seven blocks back home. Phew, that streetcar ride over the Trinity was quite an experience. I will never forget those trolley rides.

We did not live in Oak Cliff very long before we moved back to East Dallas. I was very unhappy with the way we were living our lives. There was so much change. It felt as if we were never settled.

I told my mother I was unhappy and did not want to live with her anymore. I asked if I could go live with my father. She said, "If that's what you want, okay." The next day she put me in the car and took me to my father's office. He met me and put me in his car. He and I drove back to Oak Cliff, where he and my stepmother lived. I was now starting a new life at the age of 8 and a half. I felt sure I was doing the right thing for myself. But I also felt like I was forcing myself on my father and stepmother. Nevertheless, they took me in.

CHAPTER 2

After several years of living with my father, I called to talk to my brothers. I was probably 15 years old at the time. We got together, and I found out mother had such a hard time making a living, she placed both of them in Buckner Children's Home for Orphans. They lived there for several months before Mother could take them back home.

At that time, my father and stepmother were living in an apartment, and soon after that, they bought their first house in South Oak Cliff.

I enrolled in another new school, Trinity Heights. At my previous school, I was in high third grade, which, in today's terms, would be considered the 9th grade. Because Trinity Heights did not have a high third grade, I had to go back to the low third. By now, I was two years behind in school and two years older than my classmates. Because I couldn't read, I felt like the big dummy.

Despite the problems I had at the new school, there were a few lighthearted moments. While in the fifth grade, early one morning in my first class, my friend Ricky Hatley was sitting in front of me. He turned and said, "Hey Robert, would you like some chocolate candy?"

I said, "Sure," and he gave me a big bar of chocolate. I ate the whole thing right then.

A few hours later, I became sick and upset in my stomach. I ran to the restroom and spent a whole class period there. My friend Ricky and two other boys came to the restroom to check on me, and they were laughing. Ricky told me that the bar of chocolate was actually a bar of "eggs lacks."

His father owned a drugstore, and I suppose he took it from his father's store.

For many years, Ricky liked to tell everyone the story of him giving me Ex-Lax in school, and how they had to come to the bathroom between classes to check on me. He loved to tell that story, because he thought it was so damn funny.

Outside of the few good moments I had in grade school, my reading problems seemed to be getting worse. Somehow, I made it to the 8th grade.

At Trinity Heights, 8th grade was considered grade school, while the Dallas school system considered 8th grade as junior high. So, I started attending Boude Story Junior High. I was very concerned about the upper classmen I'd encounter there. I had heard rumors about what they would do to first year students. I'm so grateful that it was only a rumor. Nothing bad happened to us.

I remember our History teacher would have each of us stand up beside our desks and read from whatever book were studying. I despised having to stand up and read. The teacher started at the end of one row of students and moved one by one down the row before starting over at the next row. Each student would stand, read, and then sit back down. The closer it came to my turn, I'd get nauseated and my whole body would start to feel numb. My legs would become so stiff, I was sure that I would not be able to stand. When I tried to read, my body seemed to freeze, and the words would not come out of my mouth. There were some words I recognized, because I'd seen them so many times, like "he," "she," "we," "you," etc. But there were many more words I didn't recognize.

Many times, the teacher would help me when I got stuck on a word, by saying the word for me. But even with this help, I still couldn't say the word. Out of the corner of my eye, I would see some of the students snickering. I was so embarrassed, I just wanted to throw the book on the floor and run out of school.

Here I was, two years older and a head taller than most of the students. I felt like I was the biggest dummy in the whole school system. Even worse, all my classmates now knew that I was dumb and stupid. What could I do? Nothing. At times like this, I would rather kick a grizzly bear in the butt than read aloud in class. At least the bear would probably eat me, and then I would never have to read again.

Oh, what a relief that would be.

In addition to the issues my reading caused me, I sometimes got in trouble for other things. When I was in the eighth grade, there were some students who rode the bus to school. Evidently, some of them would take a knife and carve up the back of the seats.

Our principal made an announcement on the PA system, saying anyone who got caught with a knife would be expelled from school. One day, while I was in study hall, I had an object that looked like a knife that I had gotten out of a gum machine. It was very small, and it was not sharp. It probably wouldn't cut hot butter, but the teacher saw it and sent me to the principal's office. He expelled me for two days and told me I would have to bring my father back with me to get back in school.

When I went home that day and told my father what had happened, he got very angry, because he knew my "knife" was just a toy.

While I was expelled, I had to go to work with my father. I had to sit next to his desk all day. It was very boring, and there was nothing to do. So, while my father was working in other parts of the building, I found a large container of paper clips to occupy myself. I clipped them all together, one by one. I thought that was fun, but I don't think my father was happy about it. The next day I got to stay home. That afternoon, when my father came home from work, he brought his large container of paper clips. He told me to separate each one of them. At that point, it wasn't as fun as it was the day before.

On the third day, my father took me to school and talked to the principal. He expressed his opinion that he thought the actions of the school were unjustified. He told him that we lived four blocks away, and I walked to school every day and did not ride the bus. Even if I did ride the bus, there was no way I could've cut those seats with a toy I got from a gum machine.

It felt good for my father to stand up for me.

The other kids, I thought, all had something they were good at, like sports or other extracurricular activities.

I desperately wanted to be known for doing something good. I guess that's why I got into so much trouble. I got into fights and started skipping school. When the pressure became too much to bear, I stopped going to school altogether. Instead of facing my demons, I got a job at a drugstore. After school, the students would come into the store and seemed to be having fun. I was certainly not having fun, so I decided to return to school.

I continued to get in trouble when I got back. To avoid punishment, I'd run away from home and catch freight trains and ride across the country. One time, I made it as far as Bakersfield, California. Over time, I became streetwise. It was amazing to me that I could learn the train schedules and track locations and destinations from the "hobos" at the freight yard.

I always returned home, though. Life was always better at home, much better than freight cars in the middle of the night. I must say, I felt terrible about causing my parents so much worry.

By then, I was going into the 9th grade, and football season was in full swing. The girls seemed to be crazy about the football players. I wanted to play football, so the girls would like me too. But there was one problem. I noticed that the football players were always walking around reading their play books. So, I knew, because of my reading problems, that I would not be able to join them on the field.

After football season came basketball season. I paid very close attention to the basketball players. I was delighted to see they weren't walking around with playbooks. Because I couldn't read, I thought that maybe I could play basketball. One day in the lunchroom, I talked to the assistant basketball coach about trying out for the team. He invited me to meet with him after school.

    The meeting did not go well. The assistant coach told me that he had spoken to the other coaches, and they all agreed not to let me try out for the team. He explained that the other coaches had heard that I smoked, stayed out late at night, and that I would be a bad influence on the team. While none of these accusations were true, I knew there was no sense trying to discuss it further. I walked out of the gym feeling devastated, wondering "How I will ever amount to anything?"

    Later in life, when I reached my adult years, I looked back on that incident. I realized that it would have helped me so much if the coaches would have offered suggestions or tried to help me, rather than push me away. Who knows what my life could have been like if had more support?

    My problems with reading were not limited to school. I remember my struggles rearing their ugly head again when I attended Sunday School. The teacher gave us Bible verses to read. My first thought was, "Oh no, not again." In order to avoid the embarrassment of reading, I'd excuse myself to go to the restroom. One particular day when I left class to go to the bathroom, I locked the door. A little boy needed to use the restroom, and he found the door locked. He really needed to get in and even pulled the door a couple of times. There was no way that I was going to come out of the bathroom and go back to class.

I felt ashamed as I listened to the boy struggle to get inside. He gave up after a few minutes. I finally left the bathroom, happy that I'd avoided reading. But when I stepped out, I discovered a puddle of urine in front of the door. I felt terrible. Because of my fear of reading, I caused that little boy to potty on the floor. I've never forgotten that incident.

Ninth grade was still considered Junior High School. It was at this time that I got kicked out of school, along with two of my friends. I honestly do not remember what we did to cause this. They sent Neal to Adamson High School and sent Wayne and me and to South Oak Cliff High School.

I remember being sent to Mr. W. P. Derek's office, the school principal. He said to me, "Mr. Cox, mark my word, you will end up in prison someday." That was a wakeup call for me, coming from the principal.

I'm happy to say that his prediction did not come true.

Being at a new school didn't mean things were better for me. In the ninth grade at South Oak Cliff, my grades were again terrible. I usually made D's and F's. However, I did very well in woodworking, bookkeeping, and drafting. I finally figured out that I was successful in classes where I used my hands.

During my senior year, I designed and built a very large gun case. It was 7 feet tall and had glass sliding doors. As I was finishing the gun case, I told my teacher, Mr. Kibler, that I wanted to put green pool table felt on the inside of the case. He thought it was a good idea.

A couple of days later, Mr. Kibler stopped by a class that I was in and asked the teacher if he could speak with me. When I stepped into the hallway, there was another man standing with him. He was Mr. Kibler's boss and in charge of all the wood shop classes in the Dallas School System. He told me that Mr. Kibler had shown him my gun case. I thought I was in trouble, but the man was proud of my work. He told me, "Robert, it is really bad taste to cover pretty wood." I understood exactly what he meant, and I've never forgotten that lesson.

Mr. Kibler later encouraged me to enter my gun case in a contest. The contest was sponsored by the Lumbermen's Association. It was held at the State Fairgrounds in Dallas. I entered the contest, and to my surprise I won third place! I felt so proud to have finally earned positive recognition. Today that gun case resides in my youngest son's home. I hope it remains in my family for many generations.

I would be remiss if I didn't mention that in junior high, I built a step stool that has lasted generations. My children, grandchildren, and now our great grandchildren are using to this day.

Gun case I built in my senior year of high school

CHAPTER 3

When I was in my last year of high school, a friend of mine had a pistol that he wanted to sell. I bought the gun and also a holster. The first thing I tried was the art of quickdraw, like I had seen the cowboys do. I liked shooting and bought bullets from a gun shop. I learned at the gun shop about two other men in the area who were practicing fast draw. So, because of that store owner, the three of us started practicing together.

One day after school, I was out in the country by myself practicing, shooting bottles and cans that were on a fence rail. I'd walk off, turn, and draw my gun just like I'd seen the cowboys in the movies. Then I'd switch and shoot left-handed. I practiced for about an hour. I felt like I was becoming an expert, until the next time I drew and shot, using my left hand. This time I felt a horrible pain run down my leg. I fell to the ground in severe pain when I realized that I'd shot myself in the leg. Wondering what had gone wrong, I realized the trigger had broken when I cocked the hammer back. Because there was nothing to hold that hammer, it snapped back down, discharging the bullet before I pulled it out of the holster.

I knew that I had to get to a hospital. But I was all by myself, and I didn't think I could drive my car, because it was a stick shift. It didn't take me long to figure out that I could change gears without using the clutch. I arrived at the hospital and found a nurse. I told her that I had accidently shot myself. She looked at me with a sour look. I was surprised by her expression. I expected her to be more sympathetic.

They called the police, but I didn't get in trouble for shooting myself. After checking my wound, the doctor gave me two choices: He would have to cut my leg open to get the bullet out, and it would take quite a while for me to recover. The second option was to simply give me a tetanus shot and place a Band-Aid across my wound. He told me that someday the bullet might work its way to the surface, and I could then pluck it out.

So, to this day, that bullet is still in my leg.

Prior to my senior year, I married my high school sweetheart; she was a sophomore. We knew that I needed to get a regular job. Both my father and stepmother worked for a major nationwide trucking company, East Texas Motor Freight (ETMF). I felt so blessed that my parents had worked there. That meant that I wouldn't have to fill out an application, which was important, since I couldn't read the questions. I truly believe that God was really looking out for me. To work for a company like this, I had to join the Teamsters Union. This organization would protect my seniority.

On my first day on the job, I learned a valuable lesson. I met another man who started the same day as I. We were both ready to punch in at the same time. I stepped up to the time clock but stopped to let the other guy go ahead of me. That cost me, because the clocked jumped a minute while I waited, giving the man in front of me a full minute's seniority. Because of that, I ended up working the midnight shift, while he was assigned the 8:00 am shift.

My first assignment at the freight line was unloading trucks. That meant I had to read the shipping labels to a man sitting on a stool between two trailers that were backed up to the dock. His job title was checker, and my responsibility was to give him the name of the company and the city for the delivery.

I dreaded this task. Of course, I still had my reading problem. The checkers would get frustrated with me because I misread the labels. I had to figure out something really quick, or I would lose my job. I told the checker that I could make his job easier if he would just give me the stack of bills of lading for the freight. I'd match the bills of lading to the addresses on the boxes and send those boxes to the various cities as labeled. I didn't have to read to do that. All the checker needed to do was drink his coffee. Believe me, he really liked the idea. That worked great for both of us. Nobody knew that I couldn't read.

Again, I had to thank God for allowing me to keep my secret for a little while longer.

IF ONLY I COULD READ

Despite accidentally shooting myself, I still wanted to practice fast draw. I had no way of knowing how fast I could actually draw. At that time, Gun Smoke was a popular western on television. At the beginning of each show, they featured Matt Dillon in the streets of town, drawing against another person. So, my thinking was that I would watch the beginning of each Saturday night show while wearing my guns. I would actually draw against Matt Dillon to gauge my speed at drawing the gun. After several weeks of practicing every Saturday night, I realized I was beating him to the draw.

I would get together with three other guys that I met at the sporting goods store. We would practice, using blanks or wax bullets, which kept us from hurting ourselves. We heard of another fast draw club in Fort Worth. We started meeting the fellows from Fort Worth and having quick draw competitions with each other. I really enjoyed this, and because of these practices, I found out I was pretty good with the gun. Again, I was finally achieving positive recognition and feeling genuinely proud of myself.

After working on the freight dock unloading and loading trucks for a little over a year, I was 21 years old. That meant that I was eligible to drive the trucks. One day I went in to see the terminal manager, Mr. Belcher. I told him that I wanted to drive and explained that I was now 21 years old. Of course, he had to check my driver's license to make sure I was of age and ready for this challenge. A month or two later, an opportunity came up for me to bid on a driving job. I was so excited, but I also realized that my reading problem could continue to haunt me. I knew that I had to come up with a plan.

By then I had learned a lot about human nature, and how people sometimes react to certain situations. Before I would leave the terminal to make my deliveries, I would approach one of the other drivers. I'd ask, "Where is this place, and where is this street?" As I had anticipated, they would look at the address on my bill of lading. Predictably, this is how they would respond: "Oh that's on Halifax Street, four and a half blocks from the terminal." This helped me learn the names of the streets without having to read.

So, during the day, while making deliveries, I would stop people on the street or stop at a little grocery store. I would place the bill of lading in front of a clerk or customer and ask them, "Do you know where this place is located?" Their natural reaction was to look at the bill of lading and say the address out loud. If they read the address but didn't know where it was, that was okay, because once I heard it, I was able to figure out where the address was located. This is how I figured out how to get my job done.

Having been born and raised in Dallas, I knew the name of the major streets and freeways. Although I could not spell them or read the name, I knew where they were located. That helped me to get around Dallas to deliver the freight. I knew that I was taking advantage of others by getting them to read the address, but I would never hurt or take from them. I simply needed help. This was the only way that I knew to keep my job and provide for my family.

The fast draw club that I helped organize was called the Dallas Gunslingers. We met with a club from Fort Worth to have quick draw contests. One of the places we met was called Cowboy Town. It was an old western town with a bank, a delivery store, a grocery store, and other shops. They would put on shows for tourists, like robbing the store, having a shoot-out in the street or robbing the stagecoach. It was located on Highway 183 in Irving, Texas. At the time, it was across from the entrance of DFW International Airport.

One particular Sunday, while we were holding a contest, a man named Dee Woolem came to Dallas. He was part of a gun show for the Daisy Air Rifle Company. He came to our contest and put on a fast draw and fancy gun handling performance. I found out that he had won the title of the "Fastest Gun Alive" at Knott's Berry Farm in California. His speed (pulling the gun out of the holster, cocking the hammer back, and firing his single action Colt 45 six shooter) was 12/100th of a second. He had an electrical timing device to keep track of this. It recorded how fast he could draw and fire his gun using blanks.

I watched him perform. It did not look terribly complicated. This sparked my interest in learning how to do more with my six-shooter. He told me that he had been contacted by a department store, E. M. Kahn & Company, in Dallas about doing some shows. Because he had so many other out of town commitments, he had to decline this offer. Dee encouraged me to let him know if I'd be interested in doing some of their shows.

IF ONLY I COULD READ

I followed up with the suggestion, and E. M. Kahn hired me to perform in two of their Dallas department stores. I started practicing what I thought they would enjoy. I ordered a timing device like Dee's to measure my draw and fire speed. Once I received it, I practiced for several days before doing the first show.

When it came time for the shows, I could draw and fire my Colt 45 single action at 14-18/100th of a second. I learned that the faster I tried to draw, the more I messed up. I found a comfortable speed that would work for me – as long as I didn't get too nervous. The truth is, I was nervous every time. After each show, I would ask myself, "Why do you get so nervous?"

I did not have an answer.

Kahn's Department Store advertisement

One day when we were having a fast draw contest at Cowboy Town, they were short a couple of employees and needed someone to go out and rob the stagecoach. I volunteered, and wouldn't you just know it, they gave me one of the biggest horses I had ever seen. So, I got on the horse, went out and waited for the stagecoach by the mesquite trees. I was instructed to let the stagecoach pass by, then ride out behind the it, chasing it while shooting my six shooter. Then I was to get the stagecoach to stop.

But when I tried this, the driver just kept going. I caught up with it and passed it while trying to stop the horse. My horse wouldn't stop, and I went past the stagecoach. When I thought the horse was going to take me all the way back to Dallas, it made a sudden stop on his own. To my surprise, this sudden stop threw me up on the saddle horn. To keep from falling off of the horse, I threw both arms around its neck. I could hear the people in the stagecoach laughing. I was so embarrassed. I finally slid off the saddle horn. I didn't even look back at the stagecoach. I told the horse "Giddy up," rode back to town and gave them their horse. That ended my career as a stagecoach robber.

CHAPTER 4

In 1961, the sport of fast draw was spreading all across the United States with clubs springing up everywhere. I learned about a very big contest being held in the old city of Tombstone, Arizona. This is where the famous Wyatt Earp was a US Marshall. I drove with three of our club members to Tombstone to compete in the contest. This was so exciting, because this was my first big competition. Wouldn't you just know that my first competitor to shoot against was the previous year's champion. Well, I lost right off the bat, but it was a lot of fun and a great experience. All of us lost our competitions, so we headed back to Dallas.

But that defeat was not the end for me. In 1962, I competed in the US Open Championship, in Houston, and won second place. I was so excited and proud of my accomplishment. I was gaining a reputation for being good at something. The trophy I received that day is still displayed in my office.

While pursuing my fast draw hobby, I still had to work and provide for my family. I must say that driving trucks and delivering freight was a very hot and difficult job at times.

I remember thinking back to my Junior High School days, about of the various things I could have done if only I could read. Who knows, maybe I could've been a teacher, a doctor, an accountant, or a salesman for a big company. Maybe I could've been a movie star, or a CEO of a large international corporation.

I'd tell myself, "Why, I could've been a four-star general, or even the president of the United States."

Unfortunately, I knew in my heart that I could be none of these. Because I could not read, trucking would have to do. But deep down, I just wanted to be like everyone else and take advantage of many other opportunities.

There was a convention in town sponsored by the Greek Orthodox Youth of America. They hired me to do a show and be part of their welcoming committee. I was to meet a trainload of delegates coming from St. Louis for the show. We were at the train station waiting for them to arrive, and it was late. When the train finally arrived, I was expected to hop on, go into the car full of delegates, and act like I was going to rob the train.

When the train was getting close to stopping, I hopped on and I fired both six shooters (using blanks) into the air while shouting "This is a holdup!"

The people did not react the way I thought typical conventioneers would react. They calmly got off the train, while the welcoming committee stood outside singing the "Eyes of Texas are Upon You." These so-called delegates just walked right on past the welcoming committee. It took a moment for us to realize it was the wrong train. A while later the correct train came in. They wanted me to hold the train up again, but I declined. The last time I tried that it was quite embarrassing.

Meanwhile, back at the hotel where the convention was held, I stepped into a café to get something to eat. While sitting at the counter in my costume, I took my cowboy hat off and placed it on the stool next to me. Shortly after that, two young ladies came in. One of them picked up my hat and put it up on the counter. I looked at her and wondered, "Why'd she do that?"

Then she said to me, "You're with the Greek convention, aren't you?"

"No," I replied. "I'm just doing a show for them."

She said, "Oh, I'm sorry, I thought you were Greek. You have such a big nose."

Oddly, that left me feeling very warm and welcome.

These experiences left an impression on me. I realized that whatever I decided to do with my life, I'd better be a good guy. After failing at robbing stagecoaches and trains, I understood that playing the bad guy didn't work for me.

In 1962, I was contacted by the Colt Patton Firearms Company. They wanted me to do a series of shows for them at the Montgomery Ward Stores in Fort Worth. They also had four engraved pistols that would be displayed during the show. The pistols had four miles of fine gold bead stamped into the engraving work. One of the pistols was a Colt 45 Buntline Special, like Wyatt Earp carried on TV. I felt very honored that Colt Patton Firearms wanted to hire me as their representative.

I knew I had to do something to stand out from the others.

Hmmm... What could do I do? I decided to buy a second gun, then I'd be a two-gun man.

Teaching myself to twirl guns

In the meantime, in 1963, I learned that Six Flags over Texas was hiring entertainers for the World's Fair in New York City. We were to work in the Frontier Palace at the Texas Pavilion. I auditioned to do my show, and they hired me. I met a lot of important people while doing that show. My supervisor at the Texas Pavilion was Mr. Michael Jenkins, who later became President and Managing Director of the Dallas City Music Hall.

When the time came to fly to New York, there were three plane loads of people working in various parts of the Texas Pavilion. There were only four of us doing shows as gunslingers. The rest were singers, dancers, waiters and waitresses.

When we arrived at the World's Fair with our guns, we learned that New York City had a Sullivan law. This meant that no one, except for the Police Department, was allowed to have a gun without a special permit. Of course, we did not have such a permit. We went to the police department to find out what to do. I remember the police sergeant asking us, "Where are your guns?" Then he stopped himself before asking the full question. I guess they would've had to take our guns, if we acknowledged having them. We were not told by the Six Flags Organization about needing a special permit to bring a gun into the city.

Thankfully, they were able to solve the problem. They hired a Pinkerton detective, which is a nationwide detective agency. The way it worked was at night, after our performance, the Pinkerton detective, Tony, took our guns to a local police station. They kept the guns overnight. The next day Tony would bring our guns to work. All of our firearms were listed under Tony's Permit. Everywhere we went with the guns, outside of the Texas Pavilion, Tony had to be with us. It worked out great. We were much safer and did not have to keep track of our guns.

At the fairgrounds, we would go outside of the Texas Pavilion to eat. I had such a distinct Texas accent that I could have made money just talking to people. For example, when we would be eating and talking, I could see people standing around nudging each other just to hear my Texas drawl.

This was just a few months after President Kennedy was shot in Dallas. One of the things we would hear was, "You folks in Texas really shoot straight."

We would come back to them with, "Yes, but you out stab us!" This comment was in reference to a news article I came across a few months prior to our arrival. A woman in New York had been stabbed by a man. While she was lying on the sidewalk screaming for help, no one would help her. The assailant came back and stabbed her again.

They told us in New York City we would have to join the union and have a booking agent. I asked them why I needed a booking agent when I already had the job. They told me the agent was going to get me on several television shows, including Johnny Carson. I just knew that it was a rip off to get money out of us. One day the booking agent came out to collect his fee. I asked him about the interview, shows, and being on the Johnny Carson show. He acted like he knew nothing about it.

In addition to this irritation, one day between shows we were told to help move a piano and other props onto the stage. I knew, from my union experience, that moving furniture and props was not my job. When the union rep came to collect his money, I complained. I told him this was stage work, and we were entertainers. He confronted the management. They told him that they had done no such thing. Unfortunately, the union rep accepted their statement and not mine.

CLIFFOLKS AT WORLD'S FAIR...

... Robert Cox, 1318 Oakley in Oak Cliff, receives his official badge as he takes over as Sheriff of the Frontier Palace in the Texas Pavilions at the New York World's Fair. Cox is presented his badge by Michael Jenkins, manager of shows in the Texas Pavilions Frontier Palace, while Miss Cookie Cage of Dallas, looks on. Both Cox and Jenkins were born and raised in Oak Cliff. Cox was hired for the Texas Pavilions on the basis of his professional ability and experience with guns. The Texas Pavilions are owned and operated by Angus G. Wynne Jr., also of Dallas.

Receiving Sheriff's badge from Michael Jenkins at the Frontier Palace in the Texas Pavilion (New York City World's Fair)

All of the Texas Pavilion employees lived in one apartment complex. There was a special bus that picked us up to take us to work at the fairgrounds. One day I complained to the others that it sounded like the people living above me were moving furniture every night. The man sitting in front of me said he was staying in the apartment above me, and it wasn't him making the noise; it was the people above him. He said he had heard the same noise. I wondered how that could be, considering the apartment we were living in was a new construction. There had to be no insulation between the floors. I wondered if all the apartment buildings in New York City were noisy like this.

On a rather humorous note, we were also told that there was horseback riding in the park close to the apartment complex. The only horse I ever saw was a policeman on horseback.

In addition to my one-man show, I would also participate in a western shoot out scene in front of the bar in the Texas Pavilion. One particular night, we had the shootout where I shot the other cowboy and then dragged him out of the palace. In the process of dragging him, I noticed that my left side felt very light. I looked down at the holster on the left side, and there was no gun. I knew instantly someone had pulled my gun out of the holster. I dropped the "dead cowboy" on the concrete floor and yelled for the Pinkerton detective. There were two bouncers, both at least 6'4", muscular and handsome. The bouncers immediately blocked off both exits and started searching everyone as they were leaving.

Was this legal? I do not know. In the process of searching people, a man walked up to us and said, "Are you looking for a gun?"

When we said "Yes," he told us that he saw a man standing at the bar that had taken the gun out of my holster.

When I started walking towards this person at the bar, one of the bouncers stopped me and said, "Let me handle this." The bouncer walked up to the man and placed his hand on his shoulder. The bouncer turned him around, placed his hands together, pushed them inside this man's jacket, and moved his hands down towards the floor – forcing the man's jacket open. My pistol was in his belt. The bouncer grabbed the pistol in a matter of seconds. This bouncer was a real professional. I'd never seen anything like it.

He took the man into the back room. I was so angry, I wanted to call the cops. We found out that this guy was on military leave. Tony, the Pinkerton detective and the bouncer said to me, "If I press charges, he would go to jail. After completing his jail sentence, the military would arrest him for being AWOL and put him in military prison. Then he would get a dishonorable discharge, which would destroy his life."

Can you believe that this thief said he thought that it was a cap gun? Anyone would have known, just by the weight of that gun, that it was real. The important thing was that I did get my gun, and I was very relieved. So I did not press charges and let him go.

That was quite an experience for me, especially watching how that bouncer worked.

Me performing at the Texas Pavilion

After being at the World's Fair for about three months, they started letting people go. Unfortunately, the Texas pavilion was losing money and could not afford to keep everyone. They let me go, and they still owed me overtime pay. Unfortunately, they never paid me. I filed a complaint with the union, and several months later I got a response from the union saying I needed to "re-file." I knew I was wasting my time, so I let it go. I took it as a learning experience.

I had so many interesting experiences while in New York. I won't mention all of them, however one in particular sticks in my mind. One day I needed to catch a taxi to go downtown. I had never done this before, but what I'd heard was to stand on the curb, watch for a cab without a passenger, and wave it down. While waiting for a cab to drive by, I noticed that an older lady had walked up behind me. She stood there for a while and eventually backed up against the building. I spotted a taxi without a passenger and waved him down. As the cab pulled over and stopped, this sweet old lady ran past me, grabbed the taxi door, opened it, jumped in, slammed the door shut, pushed the lock down, and looked at me as if to say, "You're such a dumb ass."

As I stood there in shock, watching the taxi drive off, I thought to myself, "Did I really see what I think I saw?" and "Is this way that people in NYC treat each other?"

Another strange experience I had in New York was when we went downtown to eat one day in April. I ordered tea with my meal, and the waitress screamed back at me, "Tea? It's not summertime. We don't serve tea this time of year!"

I guess drinking tea year-round must be a Texas thing.

In order to work the World's Fair, I had to take a leave of absence from my regular job. Fortunately, I was able to return to my truck driving and only lose three months of seniority.

CHAPTER 5

Now that I was starting to do more shows, I decided I needed a stage name. I had seen two other guys come through Dallas, performing gun shows. One called himself "The Fastest Gun in the West," and another, "The Fastest Gun Alive." Because I knew by now that my shows did not always turn out the way I planned, I certainly didn't want my stage name to reflect something that might not be true. So, since I was born in Dallas, I decided to call myself "The Texan."

Me driving for East Texas Motor Freight

After returning to my job with the freight line, I continued to put on gun shows at various private parties, conventions and wherever I could get bookings. One evening I was invited to perform at the Oak Cliff Junior Chamber of Commerce. I might add that I also decided to become a member. This was so good for me. Again, I was getting recognition for doing a good job, which was something I still badly needed. I was in charge of several projects, and I won state awards for outstanding leadership.

One year later, I was awarded Outstanding Jaycee of the Year. That award banquet was held in a local hotel ballroom. Afterward, several of us went downstairs to the bar. There were quite a few people there. As I was looking around at all the people, I recognized one of them, Mr. W. P. Derek, my junior high principal. I noticed that he was staring at me as if he was trying to think of where he had seen me. I had the "Outstanding Jaycee of the Year" plaque in my hand. I wanted to walk over to him and re-introduce myself, hoping he would remember my name. I wanted to show him what I had just achieved and tell him how wrong he was in judging me. I chose not to. The important thing was that I knew what I had achieved. I didn't need his validation.

Although I was doing more and more shows, I knew that something was missing. One day I heard the word *finale* and what it meant. I realized that was what I needed. My shows didn't have a strong finale. So, I started thinking about something I had never seen.

"What if I could learn to twirl both of my guns to music?"

Of all of the other people that were doing western shows, I was unaware of anyone who twirled guns to music. So, I started creating my finale. I took several musical arrangements and selected five different parts that I thought would be lively pieces to twirl my guns. I took these five different parts to a recording studio and hired them to pull them together to make one musical arrangement. The finale lasted 57 seconds. Now I was faced with yet another dilemma: "How in the world am I going to synchronize a twirling routine with both guns to this music?"

All I could think was, "Lord I need help."

I had a long practice tape made. This enabled me to have a musical arrangement long enough to practice continuously without stopping. I practiced with my guns for an hour or more every afternoon. I twirled them in different directions, in order to synchronize the gun twirls with the music. I was very proud of what I was able to accomplish, without anyone's help.

Now that I had my musical arrangement on tape, I knew it would also help if I could get an introduction of myself on the tape. That way, when performing at shopping centers, everything would be included as a complete package.

As a member of the Oak Cliff Junior Chamber of Commerce, we worked with various Metroplex Jaycee groups. In the process, I had become friends with a member of the Dallas Junior Chamber of Commerce, Johnny K. He was an announcer for WRR radio station and had a very good radio voice. After visiting with him, he agreed to not only write an introduction for me, but also to put it on tape. Now I had the introduction I needed and the music to twirl my guns. Finally, it was coming together for me.

Twirling two guns to music

IF ONLY I COULD READ

One day Johnny K called me and told me the Original Ted Mack Amateur Hour would be filming in Dallas and looking for different talent. He encouraged me to audition. I auditioned part of my show for the casting director. He changed my routine and told me to do a little skit that he created for me. Each talent had only had a minute and a half to impress him. He told me to come back next week and show him what I had done. I went home and practiced and returned the next week. He changed my routine again and told me to come back the following week. The third time I went back to audition, Ted Mack was there.

My routine included me shooting a Styrofoam cup. I was to take the cup and hold it waist-level and then drop it. I would draw my gun out of the holster, cock the hammer back, fire and burst it into little pieces before the cup dropped 12 inches. Because of my anxiety about Mr. Mack's being there, I missed the cup. I still had time left in my routine, so I just kept going.

When I finished, I turned to Mr. Mack and said, "I can hit this cup."

The casting director told Mr. Mack, "He can hit the cup. I saw him do it two other times."

Mr. Mack said to me, "I want to see you do it."

So, I picked up the cup, dropped it and blew it to pieces.

Mr. Mack said to me, "Okay, when we film the show, I want you to miss the cup the first time and hit it the second time."

That was the first indication that I would be on the show. I told myself there was no way I would intentionally miss that cup and put that kind of pressure on myself. The entire nation would be watching. I must admit that I thought, "Maybe Mr. Mack had been drinking too much of that Geritol that he had been advertising."

When we filmed the show, and I dropped the cup, I drew my gun a little slower than normal, just to make sure I hit the cup the first time and did not make a fool of myself, especially on national television.

The Texan

……..it all happens in less than quarter-second

Dropping and shooting the cup (Like I did on the Ted Mack Amateur Hour)

I could not wait to tell my father that, on Sunday afternoon, I was going to be on the Ted Mack Amateur Hour. I was so excited. I gave him the exact day and time of the airing. I just knew he'd be so proud.

My wife and I did not have a color television set, so we went over to a neighbor's to watch the show. Our neighbor had no idea I was going to be on Ted Mack, so it really surprised them when they saw me performing. Afterwards we drove out to my parents' home. I was so excited to hear what my daddy would say. When we got there, I asked him what he thought about the show. He said that they had forgotten to watch. Apparently, some of their friends came by to visit.

I thought to myself, "If that was my son on national television, there would be no way that I would miss it." I was devastated. Even at that age, I desperately needed to hear my daddy say, "Good job, son."

I felt crushed, as if whatever I did wasn't important. His response took all of the wind out of my sails, you might say. What an empty feeling. I had so many disappointments in my life, but this was a big one.

If I had won first place on the show, I would have been invited back, but I did not. The exciting thing to me was that I was exhibiting my skills on national television.

Me with Ted Mack at the State Fair in Sedalia, Missouri

A few weeks later, the Ted Mack Amateur Hour Association called my workplace to get in touch with me. While I was out making deliveries, my dispatcher called on the radio to tell me that Ted Mack was trying to contact me. I returned the call and was told they wanted me to meet Mr. Mack in Kansas City, then drive up to Sedalia, Missouri to perform at the Missouri State Fair. I felt so very honored to be invited to perform on the same stage with Mr. Mack. To me, that was better than winning first place. I have a DVD copy of that show, which aired April 16, 1967. This is something I can pass on to my grandchildren and great grandchildren.

When we filmed the show, I met a make-up artist named Peggy Taylor. She had a local booking agency for television commercials and motion pictures. After the show filmed, she asked if I would be interested in listing with her agency. She said there might be some opportunities to be in television commercials or motion pictures. I told her, "I sure would love that."

A few weeks later, Peggy called to invite me to audition for a commercial. It was a brand-new product that was coming on the market. This would allow for national exposure, if I was selected. I showed up for the audition and found that there were quite a few people there to audition. The new product was Five-day Deodorant. To my surprise, I was selected for the part!

I met a young lady who also showed up for the audition. Her car had broken down, so her father drove her. He sat against the wall waiting for his daughter. Meanwhile, the casting director told the father that he liked the way he looked. He ended up hiring him but not his daughter. It's strange how things happen.

I have to say it was exciting to see myself in a television commercial.

When I filmed the Five-Day Deodorant commercial, there was no actors' union in Dallas. So, for this national commercial I was paid a can of Five-Day Deodorant spray and $100, with no residuals.

On the set of the Five-Day Deodorant commercial

A week or so later, Peggy Taylor called me again to tell me that they would be auditioning for a WWII movie starring John Agar and Dick Webb. When she asked me if I would be interested in auditioning for a part, I said "Of course. I will be there."

I was especially excited to be auditioning for a WWII movie. I love war movies. Several days before the audition, I had fantasies, thinking that I would really look good in this war movie. Maybe John Wayne would see me and want me to be in one of his movies. I showed up at the audition so excited.

When they called my name, the first thing the casting director did was hand me a script and said, "Would you please read the script for soldier number two?"

All of a sudden, I felt like I was back in Junior High, trying to read in class. The same feelings came over my body, the stiffness and then the numb feeling. My heart raced, and I broke out in a sweat. I tried to read the script, knowing I wouldn't be able to do it. What a disaster. I felt so stupid, especially when the casting director looked at me and said, "Okay, Robert thank you."

I turned around and walked out feeling so stupid and embarrassed.

I told myself, "This is my first time to audition for a movie and it went like this."

A week or so later, Peggy Taylor called and asked if I wanted to be an extra in the movie. That meant that I would have no words to say and not be seen very much. That was okay. At least I was going to be in a movie. John Wayne would just have to wait a while for his opportunity to meet me.

When it came time for the filming, I took some vacation time. The movie was filmed at White Rock Lake, in Dallas. The director, Larry Buchanan told me to go to wardrobe and put on a German soldier's uniform. They gave me a rifle with a bayonet and told me that I was to charge and stab an American soldier. The soldier that I was told to stab was actually a cameraman. The German helmet I had on was too big and did not have a liner. It flopped up and down in front of my eyes.

Me on the set of Hell Raiders

To make things worse, the German boots I had on were way too big for my feet. As I charged the American soldier, I stepped on a Coke bottle that was on the ground in some tall grass. When I stepped on the bottle, I turned my ankle. At the same time, Dick Webb, who was the American soldier, shot me.

The director yelled, "Cut."

I got up off the ground, and the director came over to me and said, "That was great. You die good!"

When the helmet flopped back-and-forth, I hit the ground and busted my nose. What an experience.

The director then told me to go back to wardrobe and put on an American soldier uniform. As an American soldier, I got killed again.

The director said, "Go back to wardrobe and put on a German officer's uniform."

This uniform had some type of metal on it (as if the soldier had done something very important).

I thought, "Now that I am an officer, maybe they would give me some lines to say, and I would make more money."

Well that did not happen. They just continued to kill me. As I lie there with my face in the dirt, I was thinking to myself, "Is this all I will be able to do because I cannot read?" This was a major turning point.

I told myself, "I must get some help somewhere."

This movie was filmed in 1968, my very first movie as an actor. Although, I was an extra, I felt so good about it.

Me on the set of Hell Raiders

CHAPTER 6

In July 1970, I did my first promotional show for a shopping center in Dallas (Big Town). They hired me to do three shows a day on a Friday and a Saturday. They used my performance to help draw crowds into the mall. When I did my performance in the evening, the mall crowd was so large. It was unbelievable. I had no idea that so many people would come to see my performance. The shopping center advertised my performance by running ads in the local papers.

On Saturday morning, I returned to do my first performance. Because there were too many people in the mall, the manager told me he had to cancel my performances for Saturday. I felt like the fire department had something to do with this.

The mall manager that hired me, Mr. John Kimberly, said he and the merchants were very pleased with my performance, but I could not perform if the mall was too crowded. It was especially disappointing, because one of cousins had driven from Fort Worth see me in action. At least the shopping center was happy with me.

Advertisement for Big Town Shopping Center

IF ONLY I COULD READ

Southwest Shopping Center
PROMOTION COUNCIL

Mr. Robert Cox
2104 Heather Glen
Dallas, Texas 75232

Dear Mr. Cox:

I want to take this opportunity to thank you for the excellent job you did for us at Big Town as "The Texan". Your gun handling was only part of it. What really made it was the total production effort you put into it--the timing, the music and your running commentary.

I think you should be billed as the "Turnkey Texan"--because your act is so complete, it should delight any promotion director.

Sincerely

SOUTHWEST SHOPPING CENTER
PROMOTION COUNCIL

John L. Kimberly, Jr.

JLK/as

Letter from Southwest Shopping Center

If I wanted to be a movie actor, I couldn't afford to repeat my last script reading disaster. I called my booking agent, Peggy Taylor, to ask her where I could get some help. She told me about an acting class, so I went. Well, wouldn't you know, the first thing they did was give everyone a script to read. It only took two classes to realize this was not going to work for me. So, rather than make a fool of myself, I dropped out. I had to get realistic about this.

I knew it was important to focus on my script reading, but since I was getting nowhere with that, I decided to focus on my performance.

While driving trucks all over Dallas, I witnessed so much. In December 1968, while making deliveries on Coit Road, I came upon an accident. One of the cars was in flames. Unfortunately, there was a man in the car. I noticed there were several people standing around doing nothing, and I knew that he needed help to escape from the car. I ran back to my truck and got a hammer. Thank God one of the mechanics in our maintenance shop had left the hammer on the running board of my truck. I felt grateful that I had placed the hammer in the cab, because I used it to break out the window.

I was able to get the car door open and pull the man out. The ambulance came and took the man to the hospital. He gave me his wife's work phone number and asked me to call her. I called and told her that her husband had been in an accident, and he was okay. I informed her that he had been taken by ambulance to the hospital. Suddenly the phone went dead. One of her coworkers came to the phone and told me the man's wife had passed out. She had asked me for my name and the name of my employer.

A few days later, the office manager at ETMF called and asked if I had helped someone that had been in a wreck. I told him that I had, and why do you ask? He told me that the man's wife had called the company to thank me for helping her husband. A week or so later, I was contacted by Open Road Magazine. The magazine features stories about truck drivers. They asked if I'd be willing to be interviewed by a reporter regarding this incident. I told them I'd be honored. The article was featured April 1969. Coincidentally, the man I rescued was related to my cousin.

ROBERT COX

OPEN ROAD
AND THE PROFESSIONAL DRIVER
1015 Florence Street • Fort Worth, Texas 76102

Co-Publishers
WILLARD BARR
LEE GOODMAN

General Manager
R. B. HALPIN

Telephone
(817) 336-5837

January 10, 1969

Mr. Robert Cox
c/o East Texas Motor Freight
Dallas, Texas

Dear Mr. Cox:

We saw the story about you in "The Beam", and we are very interested in contacting you for an interview.

We would like come over sometime and interview you about your fast-draw routine and your heroic action in saving the man from the burning car.

Please advise us when you will be available to see us, and we would very much like to have your home address and telephone number.

Sincerely yours,

Roger Summers
Editor

RS/ch
cc:file

Letter from Open Road Magazine

IF ONLY I COULD READ

In 1971, I was contacted by one of the motion picture companies out of Hollywood to help promote a new movie that would be coming to Dallas. Its starring actor was Audie Murphy, and the title was Quick Gun. The promoters had a cap gun contest for small boys in conjunction with my gun show. This was especially exciting for me, because it was going to be showing at 11 theaters shortly thereafter. I was so hoping that I would get to meet Audie Murphy, but I never did.

Advertisement for cap gun contest

In August 1970, Peggy Taylor called me and said she was sending me to audition for a Bell Helicopter commercial. At the audition, there was no script to read, so I felt very relieved. I landed the part as a businessman. We flew from their local facility to Bridgeport, Texas. My role as a businessman was to inspect sand and gravel pits.

In October 1970, I received a call to do my gun show at a tradeshow for the American Public Works Association. I was hired by the Rockwell Manufacturing Company Flexible Pipe Division. My role was to stand in their exhibit booth and do shows. The day of the show, I drew a large crowd around the Rockwell booth. People were standing in other companies' booths to watch me perform. I found out later that several of the other exhibitors were complaining. Apparently, people were watching me and not looking at the other exhibits.

Between shows one day, I went to the restroom. I couldn't believe it; a man followed me into the restroom and said, "I didn't get to see the show. Will you put on a little show for me here in the bathroom?"

While I felt flattered, my response was, "No. I'm sorry, but you'll have to catch the next show."

IF ONLY I COULD READ

> **Flexible** PIPE TOOL DIVISION
> ROCKWELL MANUFACTURING COMPANY
>
> 415 SOUTH ZANGS BOULEVARD • DALLAS, TEXAS 75208 • TELEPHONE: (214) 946-9241
>
> October 9, 1970
>
> Mr. Robert Cox
> Dallas, Texas
>
> Dear Texan:
>
> I want to compliment you on the wonderful performance you gave at the 1970 American Public Works Association Conference held in Dallas.
>
> Your performance in fancy gun handling has been called to my attention by telephone calls and letters from all over the country. Mr. Robert Bugher, Executive Secretary of American Public Works Association, said he thought it was one of the greatest acts he has seen at any American Public Works Association Conference. In fact, he watched three of your shows during his busy time. Your act gave the real Texas and Western flavor and you have our highest recommendations.
>
> Thanks for a great show.
>
> Cordially,
>
> ROCKWELL MANUFACTURING COMPANY
>
> Gordon D. Arnold
> Sales Manager
> Flexible Pipe Tool Division
>
> GDA/bb

Letter from Rockwell Manufacturing Company

A few weeks later Peggy called me for another audition. I don't remember what the product was, only that I was very excited. I showed up at the audition, and wouldn't you know, the first thing they did was hand me a "friggin" script. Of course, those same old feelings of panic and fear came over me. I felt like I was in school all over again. I knew I wouldn't be able to read it, but I was too embarrassed to tell anyone. I started trying to read the script.

After about the fifth word, the casting director said, "Oh stop, this will never fly. Thank you for your time."

This was yet another embarrassing moment.

Two days later, Peggy called again and wanted me to audition for still work. This means taking pictures for a magazine or some type of ad. I got the part, and I felt better about myself again.

The next month I got another call from Peggy. She had another audition for me. It was for a movie called "A Bullet for Pretty Boy," starring Fabian, the rock 'n' roll singer. Somehow, I did not make a complete fool of myself this time, and I landed the part for a deputy sheriff. Again, the director was Larry Buchanan. When the time arrived to shoot a roadblock scene, he told me what he wanted me to say. I wonder if he did that because he knew I had trouble

IF ONLY I COULD READ

reading. Either way, I now had speaking part in a motion picture. The only bad thing was that I never got paid, as was sometimes the case back in those days. At least it gave me some credits and photos I could add to my portfolio for future auditions.

Me on the set of A Bullet for Pretty Boy

Me on the set of A Bullet for Pretty Boy with Fabian

One of the scenes we were shooting was in an old motel on Harry Hines Boulevard, the El Rancho Motel. This was an ambush scene in which the local police, the Texas Rangers, and, I think, the FBI was involved. When Pretty Boy Floyd and his companion walked out of the motel, we all started shooting.

A block or so around the corner, on Record Crossing, there had been an incident in one of those small grocery stores. A store owner had shot and killed someone in his store. For this reason, I suppose, the Dallas Police Department was concerned that there might be a race riot. I say this because there had been several race riots in other parts of the country. Because of this incident, there were quite a few police patrol cars in the area.

When we shot the scene, there were 12 or 14 people all firing guns at the same time. I'm sure some of the police thought World War III had just broken out. We were standing around with the director, when all of a sudden, a police car came flying into the motel. The police car nearly slammed into a camera mounted on a crane with the cameraman still on it. Both police officers came flying out of the car with their hands on their guns, ready for whatever was about to happen. It took a few seconds for the policemen to realize we were shooting a movie. Everyone was relieved this ended without anyone getting hurt.

In 1970, I got an audition for a national commercial for Alka-Seltzer, which starred the movie star George Raft. The scene was a prison lunchroom. It was shot in one of the large buildings at the at Texas State Fairgrounds. We were eating lunch, and the food was so bad that George Raft took his tin coffee cup and started banging it on the table saying "Alka-Seltzer" over and over again. Then everyone else joined in, banging on the table with their cups. The scene required a lot of people. They must have contacted one of the day labor companies for these extras.

I remember standing around before we shot the scene, and one of the men standing beside me said, "This looks like the real thing."

I did not dare ask him how he knew what a *real* prison lunchroom looked like!

One of the other principal actors in the commercial was a man named Neal Fletcher, of Fletcher Corny Dogs. Whenever I think of the Texas State Fair, I'm reminded of those delicious corny dogs. Anyway, Neal told me about an incident that happened when we finished shooting the Alka Seltzer commercial. This occurred late that night, when he went to let himself into his corny dog stand. Two policemen saw him going in and thought he was breaking into the building. They didn't know he owned the place, so they were going to arrest him. Sadly, Neal Fletcher did not have his billfold or driver's license with him. The policeman finally called the captain at the precinct, and he was able to verify Neal's identity. Interestingly, that same year Neal Fletcher celebrated 50 years of selling corny dogs at the State Fair of Texas.

A few months later, I was contacted by the management of the Seminary South Shopping Center in Fort Worth. They wanted me to do a show at a breakfast for the

IF ONLY I COULD READ

shopping center employees. At the breakfast, I met a gentleman named Mr. Justin. He owned the Justin Boot Manufacturing Company. The shopping center was going to have a Miss Cowgirl Contest, and they asked Mr. Justin and me to judge the contest. The contest would kick off the annual Fort Worth Fat Stock Show. This experience allowed me to ride in an open carriage with Miss Texas for the annual parade in downtown Fort Worth. What an experience!

SEMINARY SOUTH Shopping Center
853 Seminary South, Fort Worth, Texas 76115   WA 7-8459

Mr. Robert Cox, "The Texan"
2104 Heather Glen
Dallas, Texas

Dear Bob:

Speaking on behalf of the Seminary South Merchants Association, I would like to take this opportunity to express our complete satisfaction with your presentation. There have been compliments too numerous to mention on the excellence of your performance.

It has been, in the past, somewhat difficult to plan an entertainment that is both exciting and in keeping with "The Stock Show Days Kick-off." The problem was solved with your performance.

Thank you again. The Merchants are looking forward to a repeat performance next year.

Yours truly,

Robert L. Foster
Promotion Director

rlf/j

P. S. Mr. John Justin, of Justin Boot Co., also expressed his enjoyment of your ability with the "six gun."

Letter from Seminary South Shopping Center

Despite the positive experiences I had with acting and all the important connections I'd made, the fact that I couldn't read was a demon that continued to haunt me. More and more I knew that I had to get some help. Not knowing where to start, I decided to inquire at one of the community colleges in Dallas. I learned they had reading classes that were open to the public. "Great," I thought and signed up. I was so looking forward to finally getting some help.

But after a couple of weeks of going two or three nights a week, I knew it wasn't working. I was so frustrated, I dropped out.

By then I had two sons, Robby and Rickey. One day Robby, my oldest son, showed me his report card. The grades were terrible. I got very angry with him, because I wanted my sons to do better than I. I put my hand on his shoulder and without realizing it, I had pushed him, causing him to fall backwards onto the open dishwasher door. I felt terrible. Thinking back on this, I realize my anger was driven by my fear that he would be just like me. It was painful to know that I could not help him, because I didn't know how. I didn't even know how to help myself.

A little while later, I got call for a Bonanza Steakhouse commercial. I was so excited, because this was another ad that would be televised nationally. In this commercial, I felt like a bigamist because I had to play opposite a woman who was playing the part of my wife. In the ad, I was taking "my wife" out to dinner. Being asked to eat in a commercial was a first. They sat a plate in front of me with a baked potato and a steak. They brushed across the steak with grease, making it look like it was fresh off the grill.

Beside the steak, there were two or three small pieces of steak that were warm and ready for me to eat while filming. The girl playing my wife had experience with this. When the director said, "Cut", she took the piece of meat from her mouth and placed it in her napkin without eating it. Well, for me, I was getting free steak and being paid to eat it, so I did. A few hours later, I was sick to my stomach. I had eaten way too much steak. Boy, did I learn lesson that day!

On the set of Bonanza Steakhouse commercial

One of the great things about working for ETMF, was that I could take off on Fridays to do weekend out-of-town gun shows.

I was getting very busy, and it was getting difficult to manage my gun show scheduling. I signed with JoAnne Franks Productions, a booking agency for variety acts like mine. My first booking with JoAnne Franks Productions was at the Shepherd Mall in Oklahoma City. Because this isn't far from Dallas, I decided to drive. The first show was on Friday. I was so pleased that there were more spectators than I had expected. The rest of the shows on the weekend were also well attended. I felt confident that I had done a good job drawing crowds to the shopping center.

The crowd had no idea of how many hours I had to practice in my garage each day, especially after driving, unloading, and loading trucks. My practice sessions consisted of:

- Dropping a silver dollar and shooting it before it hit the floor.

- Dropping a cup and trying to hit and burst the cup before it fell 10 to 12 inches

- Practicing on the electrical timing device (Trying to maintain the speed I needed to draw against another person)

Me performing at the Shepherd Mall

Sometimes I'd call for a volunteer to illustrate how fast I could draw. I'd draw my other six-shooter, cock the hammer and hand them the gun. I'd warn them that it had a hair trigger, and it would discharge easily. I would instruct them to watch my hand, which was about 6 inches from my gun, un-cocked in the holster. I would tell them, "When you see my hand move towards my gun, just touch the trigger. I will draw my gun out of the holster, cock the hammer, and fire my gun before you can fire yours."

The electrical timing device recorded 1-100th of a second between the two shots. With this electrical timing device, the audience could actually see the difference between my shot and theirs. I must say that no one has ever beaten me. Also, I learned that women's reflexes are faster than men.

If I was doing a show for an event where alcohol was consumed, things were a little different. If the volunteer from the audience had a few drinks, I really looked fast. After a few drinks, the volunteer's reaction time was much slower than normal. My shows usually lasted 30 minutes.

Letter from the Shepherd Mall Merchants' Association

Another thing that gave me the edge over the volunteers was my familiarity of my weapons. If I picked up a brand-new gun from the factory, I couldn't begin to do what I normally did in the shows. I needed to alter all the working parts inside of the gun. I would take my guns apart many times, file and polish each individual working part. This allowed me to be as fast on the draw as possible.

In addition to this, I had to do quite a bit of alteration on the trigger, to be able to twirl the guns around my finger and keep them from flip-flopping. This allowed me to spin them in and out of the holsters and stay in sync with the music.

Once I was hired to perform for a convention of patent lawyers. My holsters were starting to wear out and become flimsy. I needed them to be stiff. The right holster was critical for me to pull my gun with any speed at all. I was told to soak the holster or at least get it very wet and somehow heat it. This would make it stiff again. I took the advice, but I only had a few hours before showtime. I soaked my holster in water and placed it in the oven for a few minutes. I checked on it and found it still pretty wet, so I waited a few more minutes. When I opened the oven this time, I said, "Oh no, my holster resembles a piece of bacon!"

It had drawn up so much, my gun wouldn't fit all the way in it.

One rule in show business is, "The show must go on," so I drove to the hotel wondering, "How in the world is this going to turn out?"

Again, I cried out, "God, it's me again, and I need help."

When I arrived at the hotel, I stood in the ballroom in front of a very large crowd wondering what type of excuse I could make to get out of this. I decided honesty is the best policy. I told the audience the truth about what had happened. I heard resounding laughter and felt so stupid. To my surprise, the show did go on, and it turned out extremely well, in spite of my gun not fitting all the way into the holster. Even still, I will never try that again. After the show, I had to make myself a new set of holsters. My biggest problem was finding someone to sew through that leather. I visited many places and ended up at a saddle maker.

CHAPTER 7

In 1973, Peggy Taylor, my agent, called me for an audition for a movie to be shot in Dallas. Thankfully, I was able to stumble through a very short script. I landed parts for two different characters. I played Leroy, an automobile mechanic. The other role was for me to perform my usual gun show routine at a carnival scene. The movie was about dirt track racing, starring Robert Blake, Pat O'Neill, and Chris Conley, one of the stars from the series Peyton Place.

IF ONLY I COULD READ

Me and Robert Blake

The working title was called, "Going All Out." It was changed to "Corky," who was the character Robert Blake was playing. In one of the scenes, Corky got mad at our "boss" Patrick O'Neill for firing him. The scene was a drive-in café next to the garage where we worked. In the nighttime scene, Corky shot at a passing car and hit the driver. The stunt man who drove the car asked the director, "How many times do you want me to roll the car?"

The director responded, "Oh, can you give me three rolls?"

The stuntman rolled that car exactly three times. I was amazed. At the same time, I was walking out with my coworker to get in my pickup to go home. As my coworker was getting into the truck, Corky shot him, and he fell to the ground. There was so much noise coming from a drive-in café that I could not hear the gunshot. Not seeing my coworker, I slid across the seat of the truck to the other side, looking for my coworker. I saw him lying on the ground. I got out of the truck. and Corky tried to shoot me.

They had some, I guess expert shot from Hollywood, shoot a grease gun at me while I was coming out of the truck. The grease was supposed to hit the frame of the door that goes around the window and right by my head. I was very nervous about this scene. I was scared that he may hit me instead of the door frame. So, I had terrified look on my face when I came out of the truck. The shooter was standing 20 feet away when he shot, and he hit right where he was supposed to. Most everyone on the set got a great belly laugh about how I reacted. But now I knew that this guy was a very good shot. The grease that hit the truck door really looked like a real bullet had actually chipped the paint.

When the movie was released, I was disappointed. Some of the scenes I was in were totally cut out. Also, they must not have liked the sound of my voice, because they dubbed over it. I did receive residual payments over a period of a few years. The last check I received was on February 6, 2001 for the huge sum of $57.45.

A Scene from Corky with Pat O'neal

Me on the set of Corky

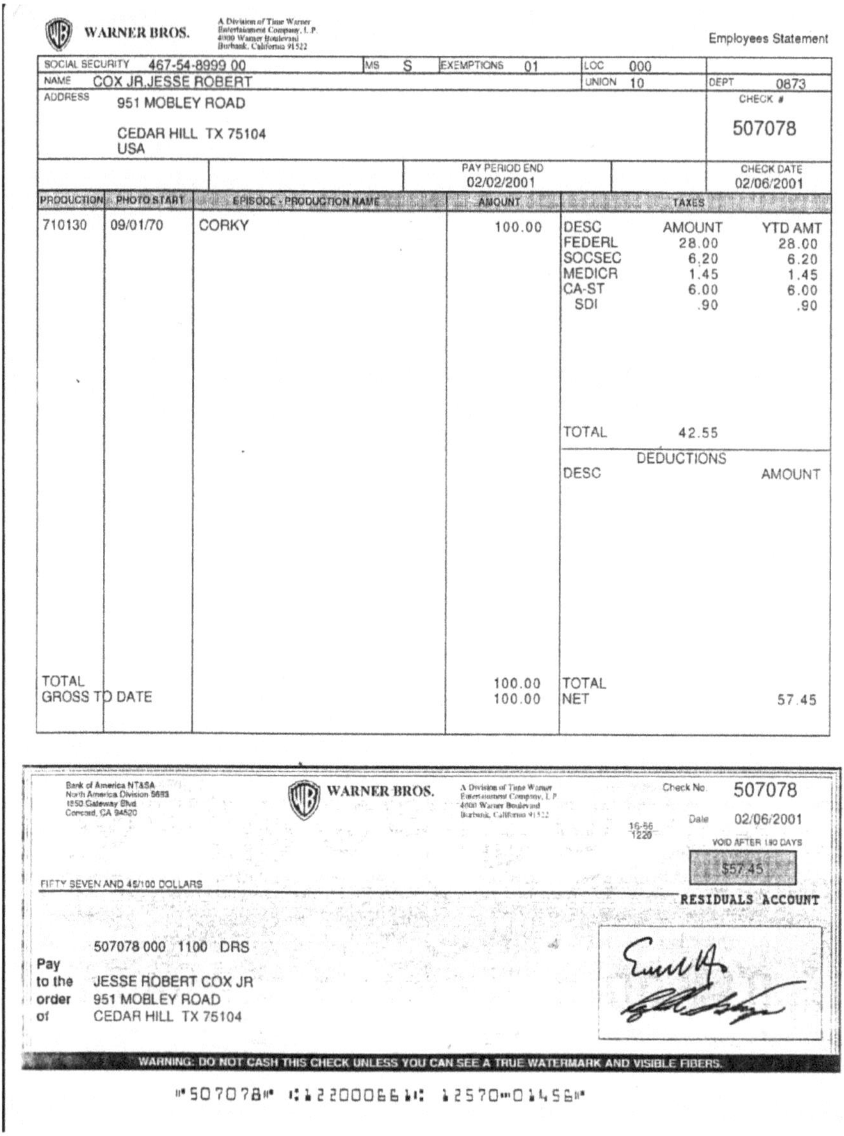

WARNER BROS. A Division of Time Warner Entertainment Company, L.P. 4000 Warner Boulevard Burbank, California 91522

Employees Statement

SOCIAL SECURITY 467-54-8999 00	MS S	EXEMPTIONS 01	LOC 000		
NAME COX JR,JESSE ROBERT			UNION 10	DEPT 0873	
ADDRESS 951 MOBLEY ROAD CEDAR HILL TX 75104 USA				CHECK # 507078	
		PAY PERIOD END 02/02/2001		CHECK DATE 02/06/2001	

PRODUCTION	PHOTO START	EPISODE - PRODUCTION NAME	AMOUNT
710130	09/01/70	CORKY	100.00
TOTAL			100.00
GROSS TO DATE			100.00

TAXES

DESC	AMOUNT	YTD AMT
FEDERL	28.00	28.00
SOCSEC	6.20	6.20
MEDICR	1.45	1.45
CA-ST	6.00	6.00
SDI	.90	.90
TOTAL	42.55	

DEDUCTIONS

DESC	AMOUNT
TOTAL NET	57.45

Bank of America NT&SA North America Division 5683 1850 Gateway Blvd Concord, CA 94520

WARNER BROS. A Division of Time Warner Entertainment Company, L.P. 4000 Warner Boulevard Burbank, California 91522

Check No. 507078

16-66 1220 Date 02/06/2001

VOID AFTER 180 DAYS

$57.45

FIFTY SEVEN AND 45/100 DOLLARS

RESIDUALS ACCOUNT

507078 000 1100 DRS

Pay to the order of JESSE ROBERT COX JR 951 MOBLEY ROAD CEDAR HILL TX 75104

WARNING: DO NOT CASH THIS CHECK UNLESS YOU CAN SEE A TRUE WATERMARK AND VISIBLE FIBERS.

⑈507078⑈ ⑆122000661⑆ 12570⑈01456⑈

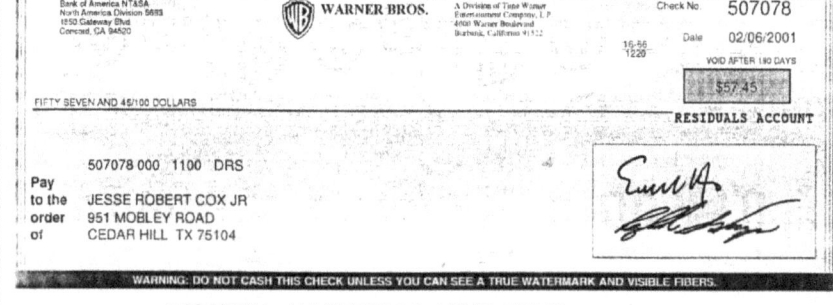

My last residual check for Corky

     I received a call from JoAnne Franks Productions with a request for shows in a Shreveport, Louisiana mall. The mall manager lined up interviews with a newspaper, television and radio station. When we showed up for the interviews, my timing device did not work. I panicked, and the mall manager was very disappointed. I do not remember how, but we found someone to work on the device and correct the problem. So, the full show went on as planned, and the crowds were large and very pleased. The mall management was thrilled.

IF ONLY I COULD READ

Shreveport Journal

THURSDAY, MAY 17, 1973   D ONE

'I've Had It!' —
Cox — A Sad Bad Guy

By JUA NYLA HUTCHESON
Journal Staff Writer

What happens to a bad guy — cowboy type — who always screws up? He becomes a good guy.

At least, that's what happened to The Texan, a quick-draw e x p e r t from Dallas named Robert Cox who goofed on every villanous job he acquired.

THE F I R S T GO-ROUND was a bit part in a World War II flick. Cox was to portray a German soldier.

"We'd been on location two weeks and all I had done was sit around, eat and get fat. Then the director was ready for me. I was to run down this long hill and b a y o n e t an American soldier," he explained.

"THE SOLDIER WAS a cameraman, lying flat on his back shooting up as though he were the soldier, and I was supposed to put the bayonet under his arm.

"This German helmet I was wearing didn't have a liner, so it kept flopping down over my eyes. And the boots were so big there was no support in the ankles.

"WELL, I TURNED my ankle and the helmet slid over my eyes and I darn near killed that cameraman with the bayonet! I didn't quite hit him but I was close enough to shake him up — and break my nose," Cox said wryly. "That was embarrassing.

"I'm just not succesful as a bad guy. I was hired to rob a train full of conventioneers in Dallas. The train was coming from St. Louis and I was supposed to jump on the moving train, run through yelling and firing my guns in the air, jump off and then a welcoming committee would sing as they got off the train. Fine.

"I J U M P E D on, ran through like I was supposed to, but they didn't react like conventioneers should. So I fired a couple of more shots while they were screaming and crawling under seats and then I got off.

"As they got off the train the committee sang 'The Eyes of Texas.' Those people just kept going. We had the wrong train. They matched me to the right one, but I said, 'forget it. I'll sing with the rest of you.' "

ANOTHER TIME, Cox was supposed to rob a stagecoach in a Western town.

"I was hiding out in the bushes with a new horse — a real monster — waiting for the stage to come by. That horse and I took off after the stage, and I was firing the gun, and then the stage coach stopped and my horse wouldn't — at least not when he was supposed to.

"RIGHT AFTER WE passed the stage, that horse put on the brakes. I had my reins in one hand and the pistol in the other." That time when the horse stopped, Cox didn't . . . . at least not when he should have.

(Journal Photo by Don Graham)
Reins in One Hand . . .
Pistol in the Other

his neck, and then, there I was, sitting on the saddle horn," he said f l i n c h i n g. "That was the last of my 'bad guy' roles, I'd had it!"

The Texan, who never calls h i m s e l f the "fastest gun" because "anybody can have a bad day," said he became interested in guns as a child.

"YOU KNOW, most kids play cowboys and Indians. Well, I just never grew up." He said he tried fast drawing and then joined a fast-draw club, traveling a c r o s s the country for c o m p e t i t i o n meets.

After appearing on the Ted Mack Amateur Hour, he was contacted by an agency and was soon doing national television commercials, m o v i e s, conventions and other appear-

Article from the Shreveport Journal

At this time, I changed booking agents and went with the Joy Wise agency. In 1973, my first commercial with Joy Wise was for Lonestar Beer. We shot it in an outdoor gazebo in Waxahachie, Texas. The main actor in this commercial was a man named, I believe, Jim Hunter. He and Burt Reynolds starred in The Longest Yard, a movie about a prison football team.

In the commercial, we had a large bathtub full of Lonestar Beer, along with beautiful hanging baskets. The director decorated the gazebo with his own plants. Between scenes, the director would go over and talk to each of the plants in the baskets. He said he did this all the time, and that's why the plants were so large and beautiful. I assumed it worked. I thought to myself, "I must try that."

I don't remember if I actually started talking to my plants though.

IF ONLY I COULD READ

On the set of a Lone Star Beer commercial with Jim Hunter

At this time, reading was still a struggle for me, but I never gave up trying. I tried to read a book about the old west and found myself frustrated and getting a headache from the strain of trying to figure out the words.

So, in 1976 I returned to the community college. I didn't know where else to go. I gave the reading classes another try. Again, I could not make any headway. I didn't know how to explain my problem to the teacher, because I did not understand it myself. I felt hopeless. I also felt thankful that God had provided me with a job that paid a decent salary and provided medical insurance. I knew it was a blessing to have this job, considering I still couldn't read.

On June 17, 1976, my birthday, I performed at the Battlefield Mall in Springfield, Missouri. While doing my show, I talked about a lot of the cowboys from the old west.

In addition to twirling both guns to music and showing how fast I could draw the guns, I added several tricks to my show. I told jokes and talked about how times have changed since the day of the old cowboys. I mentioned how long it took the old settlers to travel from Dallas to Springfield. I'm sure their journey took several weeks. But today I just hop on an airplane and fly up in a matter of an hour or two.

IF ONLY I COULD READ

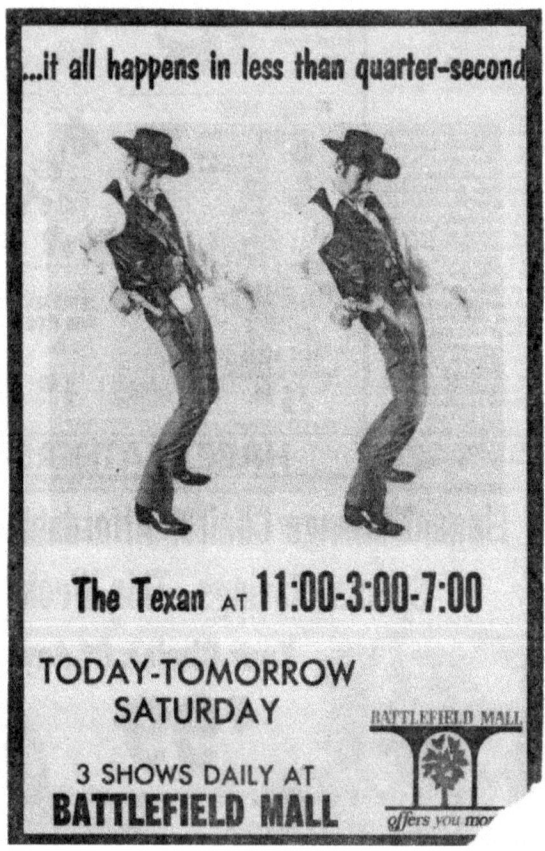

Advertisement in The Springfield Daily

At the end of each show, I would hand out autographed pictures for the audience. After one of my performances, a lady came up to me and said she had grown up in Dallas and went to school there. She had two sons with her. She told me that her husband wanted to see my show but could not get off work. She invited me to her home to have dinner with her family, so I could meet her husband. I accepted the invitation. That was so kind and generous of them. I was grateful not to have to eat in a restaurant.

On July 4th, 1976, I was performing at the Jamestown Mall in St. Louis, Missouri. The mall always ran newspaper ads to advertise my performance. The newspapers and TV stations came out to interview me. After all, how many times, especially in this day and age, does a gunslinger come to town, especially one that can twirl six shooters to music?

After one of my performances, a man named Bob Argenbright came up to me and introduced himself. Bob told me that he had read about me in the newspaper and had seen the television interview. He had heard that I was performing at the mall, and he really wanted to see me perform because he was writing a book on the fastest guns alive. He wanted to interview me and asked if he could put my picture and story in this book. I was flattered. I told him I would love to see myself in that book. About a year later, I received a copy of the book, which is in my office today.

IF ONLY I COULD READ

Advertisement for Jamestown Mall in St. Louis Missouri

One day I received a call from my booking agent, Joy, about another movie that was being filmed in Waxahachie. Thank goodness I did not have to read a script. They told me I was going to be a bailiff in a court room scene where a prostitute was going to trial for something. The prostitute got very angry in the courtroom, and I was forced to try and control her as she fought me.

This was the first time I was expected to be physical with anyone, especially a woman, in a movie. The working title was "Stamp Out Fair Play." It was about gambling back in the early 30s. If the movie ever came out in theaters, I was not aware.

Joy called again and had a Conoco Service Station audition for me. There was no script to read, and I was so relieved to get the part. It was actually filmed at a Conoco Service Station a few blocks from my home. The advertisement boasted that if a customer bought a certain number of gallons of gasoline, he or she would receive rolls of Christmas wrapping paper. We shot this a few weeks before Christmas. Two weeks later, I drove by the station

IF ONLY I COULD READ

where we filmed the commercial. I saw several cars were lined up to get gas and, I assume, Christmas wrapping paper. It felt so good to know the commercial had worked.

Conoco Service Station Commercial

Despite my success as a part-time actor, the frustration of not being able to read was really wearing me down. There were so many interesting stories I would have loved to read, stories about the Civil War and World War II. There was just so much history I wanted to read about and understand. I felt defeated that I might not ever get to read these books.

I longed to know more about WWII in Europe. My uncle Japtha had landed in Normandy on D-Day with the Ninetieth Division under General Patton. He fought all the way through Europe and managed to return home uninjured. I knew that my uncle had been involved in several major battles, like The Battle of the Bulge at Bastogne. I wanted to tell my sons, grandsons, and great grandsons about their family history. Also, now that I was a professional entertainer, I wanted to tell my audience about some of the famous men in the old west. I desperately wanted to be able to read about these people, so I could speak about them accurately.

CHAPTER 8

In 1977, I heard about a lady that could help people with reading. She worked out of her home. I contacted her and set up appointment to get some help. She lived in North Dallas. This was a long way from where I lived, but if she could help me, it would be worth the drive. I met with her and worked with her over the next several weeks. Again, I found myself getting more confused. When I realized I was getting nowhere, I told her I appreciated her help, but it wasn't working. It hurt to fail again, but I decided to stop seeing her.

I remember so many times I'd ask myself the same questions: How and where do I go to get help? Is there is any help for me?

I was so sick and tired of feeling dumb and stupid. I just knew that I was the only person like this.

A few months later, I heard on the radio that the Dallas Public Library was holding classes to help people learn how to read. After so many failures, I almost didn't bother looking into it, but I was desperate for answers. I could not bear living my life without reading. I felt like there had to be help for me somewhere. I called the library to find out which locations would have the classes. I attended the classes and met a very nice gentleman who was willing to work with me. Unfortunately, after a few nights of going to the library, it still was not working.

So again, I stopped going.

A little while later, I received a call from my booking agent, Joy. She wanted me to shoot a commercial for Mohawk Tire Company. This time I didn't have to audition. There was no script involved, and that was great. Plus, the location for the shooting was just three blocks away from where I was working. Joy had called me at about 10:30 am, while I was working. I called my dispatcher and told him I was sick and needed to go home. I drove three blocks to the warehouse where the Mohawk Tires were stored. It only took about three hours to shoot the commercial, and I had the rest of the day off.

Every 13 weeks, I received a residual check for this commercial. It ran for six and a half years. It ran only in Nashville, but I was so very grateful for being able to make that money.

One day in August 1977, I received a call from JoAnne Franks Production. They had a contract for me to do my show at the East Hills Shopping Mall in Saint Joseph, Missouri. When I did these shows, I always felt so good about myself. I was happy to be doing something that very few others were doing or could do. I did not have to worry about reading anything, and the audiences did not know my secret.

People would ask me to autograph my pictures for them. I'd have to ask the person how to spell their name. Again, my streetwise experience came in handy. I had a standard statement that I could write, after much practice at home. I'd write, "Best of luck to you and thank you for coming." Then I would sign, "the Texan." People are strange sometimes. There were times where women would want me to write something to make their boyfriends or husbands jealous. I'm not crazy and wanted no part of that.

Me signing autographs at the East Hill Shopping Mall

IF ONLY I COULD READ

ST. JOSEPH NEWS-PRE

(2d Cl. Post Pd. at St. Joseph, Mo.)   ST. JOSEPH, MO., FRIDAY EVENING, AUGUST 5, 1977

Matt Dillon on TV provided practice for fast-draw expert

By JIM DAY

The menacing pair of chrome-plated Colt .45s that dangle from the Texan's hips are the authentic Peacemakers, but Robert Cox's only aim is to entertain the townsfolk with a little fast-drawin' and gun-twirlin.'

The fast-draw artist from Dallas is appearing in three performances daily through Saturday at the East Hills Shopping Center mall.

"My best trick, and it's not really a trick because there's nothing rigged about it, I nicknamed baseball," he said. Cox places a styrofoam cup on the back of his hand held at gunbelt level. Within a fraction of a second, he drops the cup, cocks and fires his revolver, breaking the container before it falls past the tops of the lanky Texan's boots, tops.

"It doesn't work everytime, in fact, after three strikes, I'm out," he commented.

Cox performed the routine when he auditioned for the Ted Mack Amateur Hour. "I was nervous, and on the first try I missed, but after the audition was over, I told them I could do it and showed them," he said.

"The first indication I had that I would be on the show was when Mr. Mack asked me to miss the first time when I appeared on camera. I couldn't do it; I was too nervous to take a chance— I broke it on the first shot."

The Texan doesn't use live ammunition in his acts. He loads blanks in the cylinder. "It's the force of the blast that breaks the cup, but you have to aim the gun just as carefully as you would with bullets," he explains.

Cox makes appearances throughout the United States, traveling approximately 50,000 miles a year. He's also performed in several Warner Brothers and Metro-Goldwyn-Mayer motion pictures, and made television commercials for drug companies, tire manufacturers, brewers, and bakeries.

"I like working in shopping centers, although I also appear at conventions, but some strange things can happen at conventions," he remarked.

"One time I was hired to help welcome a train car of delegates coming to Dallas for a convention. As the train pulled into the station, the plan called for me to jump on the delegates' car, run through it with my guns out, making them think it was a holdup.

"When the train finally came, it was late, I ran in, my guns bangin' away. But halfway through I got the feeling something was wrong from the look on their faces. I just ducked my head and ran on through." Cox said that not only had he "held up" the wrong car, but the wrong train. Cox's interest in gunplay goes back to his youth. "Every Saturday night I'd try to outdraw Matt Dillon on the opening of Gunsmoke. Eventually I could," he said. He went on to form a fast-draw club with several of his friends, and after seeing a quick-draw artist perform in his hometown of Dallas, Cox decided to make money with his greased-lightning draw.

Was this affable gunslinger born 80 years too late for his time? "Oh no! Back in them days it was dangerous," he said.

News-Press photo by STEVE SLATER

Our "fast draw" artist — News-Press cartoonist Jim Day, left — interviews another "fast draw" artist, Robert Cox.

Article in the Saint Joseph's News-Press

ROBERT COX

August 6, 1977

Mr. Robert Cox
"The Texan"

Dear Bob:

Just a note to let you know how much we enjoyed your performances in the Mall at East Hills Shopping Center. Our first surprise came when we had good crowds for all three shows on a Thursday, which is normally not a good day for decent crowds. And the performances and the crowds were outstanding both Friday and Saturday.

We were all delighted at how fast the pictures of you were taken by the eager hands of the children, and some adults in the audience. And, of course, having our emblem on the pictures will give us publicity for years to come.

It was a delight to work with you, and I hope we can get together again sometime in the future.

Warm regards,

Vern

Vern Pepp, ASPD
Promotion Director

EAST HILLS SHOPPING CENTER · ST. JOSEPH, MO. 64506 · PHONE 279-5667

Letter from the East Hills Shopping Center

In September of 1978, I had a contract to perform at the Westland Mall in Columbus, Ohio. A few days before I left for Columbus, I got a call for a Moore Business Forms

IF ONLY I COULD READ

audition. This was not a commercial. It was what we call a still shot for a magazine or other type of advertisement. We shot the still work for Moore Business Forms the day before I left for Columbus, Ohio.

Moore Business Systems advertisement

The next morning, about 7:30 am, Joy called to say they had a problem with the pictures we took the day before and wanted to re-shoot that morning. I was horrified, not knowing what to do. I had to catch my flight at 2 o'clock that afternoon. I told Joy about the spot I was in. She arranged for the shoot to take place at 9:30 that morning, so I said okay. On the way there, I prayed we could do it in time for me to catch my flight. I was so grateful that I was able to re-shoot and catch my flight in time.

I really enjoyed doing shows for shopping centers, because of the many people who came to see me. I felt fulfilled, because each time I drew a large crowd to the mall, I was successful at doing what I was hired to do.

IF ONLY I COULD READ

Article from The Columbus Dispatch

One particularly rainy day in 1978, I was making deliveries in DeSoto, a south Dallas suburb. The rain was coming down so hard it was difficult for me see. When it stopped raining, I saw boards and other debris flying through the air. I was able to pull into a shopping center parking lot to call my dispatcher. He told me to get out of the truck before something bad happened. I do remember hearing that in the case of high winds or a tornado, to find the lowest spot and go there. I looked around and spotted a Texaco Service Station on the corner. I also saw a low-lying drainage ditch in the street and thought it would be a good place to seek shelter.

I remember placing my hand on the door handle when suddenly I heard a loud bang, and I started bouncing around in the cab of the truck. My knees were down between the clutch and the brake pedal, and my feet where back under the seat. I was covered in glass. The back of the truck was somehow sitting on the trunk of a parked car. It took a few minutes for me to realize that my truck was on its side.

I thought, "Oh no, another warning letter."

Warning letters are issued for any negative on-the-job incidents. Three warnings were considered grounds for termination. I had to climb up to get out of the door on the passenger side. I dropped down from the truck and stood there still wondering, "What just happened?" I looked around for the perfect low spot I'd spotted earlier. Unfortunately, the roof from the filling station was now covering the ditch. I stood there bewildered when someone came up to me, grabbed my shirt sleeve, and told me to come with him to a nearby flower shop. There were already several other people taking refuge there. We all got into the cooler where the flowers are stored. That incident was all such a blur. I do not even remember walking from my truck to the flower shop.

    I do remember standing there, looking out the windows of the flower shop, and I noticed the skies were black. The others were saying another tornado was getting ready to hit. Meanwhile police cars and fire trucks were driving back-and-forth, up and down the street. I was horrified, and there was nowhere to run. All I could do was stand there and visualize what had just happened, knowing that it could happen again.

    Thankfully, there was not another tornado. I called my dispatcher to tell him to send a wrecker to pick up my truck. I was very shaken, to say the least. While waiting for the wrecker, the newspapers showed up to take photos and report the story. It's amazing how reports get twisted once they get in the newspaper. One of the newspapers reported that I was on Interstate 45 when my truck was picked up. I was actually 13 to 14 miles from Interstate 45. The other newspapers got the story straight.

Looking back on the day's events, I realize God prevented me from opening the driver's side door. If I had opened that door, I could easily have lost my life.

Article about the tornado that flipped my truck

IF ONLY I COULD READ

I still had a desire to do motion pictures and television commercials, but more importantly, I knew that I needed to overcome my reading problem. It was so painful to know that I needed help and have no idea where to get it. This secret felt like a noose around my neck, and I was so very stressed. I decided to try community college again to see if I could make some progress. At the very least, I wanted to understand my problem. I signed up again, and I was assigned to a learning skills class.

Again, it did not work. I had no choice but to drop out. No matter where I turned, I continued to run into walls. Now what was I going to do? This was so overwhelming, but I couldn't quit, not after all of this.

I received another call from the booking agency about an audition that had a weird name. Can you believe the working title was "The Pickle Goes in The Middle?" I was fortunate to get a small part, in which I was cast as a Dr Pepper delivery man, delivering soda to a restaurant. This was another movie that, as far I know, never came out. I came to understand that this happens quite a bit in the motion picture industry.

In July 1978, I had a contract with a shopping center in Madison, Wisconsin to perform for three days, three shows times per day. One of the things the shopping centers seem to like about my shows was that I had my own sound system and my entire introduction on tape. This saved them a lot of work, and it was so simple for them to have me come in and set up my own equipment and then perform.

My early show at 1:00 pm was small, as expected. As usual, afterwards I signed autographed pictures. I noticed there were two children with Down syndrome in the audience. They each wanted a picture and to ask me questions about the guns and how long I had been performing. I had never been around Down syndrome children before, and I was surprised by their level of questioning.

At the 4:00 pm show, these same two boys, and a few more just like them, were there. After that show, the boys

IF ONLY I COULD READ

hung around and asked more questions. I loved it. They all laughed after receiving a picture.

There was a large crowd at the 7 o'clock show. I noticed that on one side of the stage, those same boys plus several more were there again. They were genuinely happy to be there, and I was thrilled to have them. They all seemed to be functioning well without supervision. They must have lived in a group home somewhere close to the shopping center.

Advertisement in The Window

Down deep, I knew that there had to be help out there somewhere for my reading problem. I figured either there was help for me, or I was too stupid to realize it was hopeless. So, I went back to the community college to give it another try. Every time I signed up for whatever help I could get, they'd have me take a test to determine my reading level. This time I had a male teacher that gave me the test. When I asked about my reading level, his reply was one that I'd never heard before.

He said, "Mr. Cox, you have a lot of opportunities."

I understood exactly what he meant: I wasn't stupid, I just need a lot of help.

After a few nights of going to the college classes, I realized that again I was getting nowhere. Why should I continue to put myself through this?

I dropped out again.

CHAPTER 9

One bright and sunny day in 1980, I was in downtown Dallas delivering freight. I ran into a man, Larry, that had worked at East Texas Motor Freight Line several years before. He was about the same age as I was and had worked in the office. Quite often he would be out on the docks where we worked, so I knew him fairly well. He asked me if I was still doing gun shows and TV commercials.

I told him, "Yes, whenever I can."

He told me that he was with a company that was producing TV commercials and asked if I would like to audition for one.

I said, "Of course," and gave him my booking agent's information.

A few months later, I received a call from Joy, my booking agent. Larry, the casting director, had called and asked for me to audition as a forklift driver for 7-Eleven. My response was, "Great, I won't have to read a script."

I went to the audition with my portfolio of photos and newspaper articles. There were several others in the room waiting to audition. The audition room door was open, so there were no private auditions.

When my turn came, Larry said, "Robert we have changed your part to supervisor, and here's your script."

Oh no. My body froze, and there I was, back in junior high school. I was so nervous, I felt like I would throw up. I tried to read my script, and once again, it was an absolute disaster.

I had given Larry my portfolio, and he looked through it while I was attempting to read the script. I told him, "I don't do well with cold reading."

He said, "Yes, I can see that. Did you actually do all of this?"

He was insinuating that I had fabricated my portfolio. I was doubly surprised because he knew me from previous commercials. There I stood, looking at the others, knowing that they had witnessed my disaster. They must have

IF ONLY I COULD READ

thought, "Now I've got a chance." I picked up my portfolio and handed the script to Larry.

I walked to my car, threw my portfolio on the floor, screamed and started crying.

"Why does it have to be this way?" Where is that grizzly bear when I need to kick his butt. This was a huge turning point for me. I knew I could not go through something like this again. I called Joy and told her to stop sending me to auditions that required reading. I knew that I'd have to stick to non-speaking parts.

At least I had fulfilled part of my dream.

I finally accepted that I would not able to make my living in the entertainment business. At the same time, I was so grateful that my job at the freight line enabled me to provide for my family.

During this time, I was attending a Baptist church. The Baptist Association had a program for boys called the Royal Ambassadors. It was similar to The Boy Scouts of

America. One of the members of the Royal Ambassadors asked if I would give my Christian testimony and perform a gun show for the boys. I agreed and spent a few days putting my testimony together and planning my act.

After my performance, the word spread to other Royal Ambassador Programs around the country. They called and requested that I perform for their state Royal Ambassador Congress. This was exciting because I felt like the Lord was leading me. After doing several shows in different states, I received a phone from someone who had requested me. He told me that he was not in favor of my coming after all. I was so confused. He went on to explain that he had received my brochures the year before. Even though others on the board wanted to hire me, he could not imagine how a person could take a gun and talk about Jesus Christ. Fortunately, he was outvoted by the other members and invited me to come, and I did.

I felt anxious about how this gentleman was going to feel after the show and hearing my testimony. While taking me back to the airport, I asked him for any constructive criticism that he might have. I was sitting on pins and needles, expecting to hear something negative.

Instead he said, "Robert if I hadn't seen the show and the way you took your guns and talked about Jesus Christ, I would've never believed that it could be done. I'm very glad we had you come."

Boy did I feel relieved. And I was confident that the Lord had given me this talent and was using it for His glory.

Interestingly, after a few months, the requests for shows from the Royal Ambassadors stopped, and I didn't understand. I was concerned that I had misunderstood God's will for the gun shows. I thought that the Lord was never pleased about the gun shows and stopped me. To this day, I'm not sure why I wasn't invited to do more shows.

Maybe someday I will find out.

Advertisement for The Royal Ambassadors

IF ONLY I COULD READ

Louisiana Baptist Convention
EXECUTIVE BOARD
MISSIONS DIVISION

Baptist Men and Boys Department
John T. Winters, Director
Cal Jones, Associate Director

Don F. Mabry, Director

January 25, 1980

Mr. Robert Cox
330 Robin Hill Lane
Duncanville, Texas 75137

Dear Robert:

Thank you again for coming to our 1979 Royal Ambassador Congress. Your presentation was just what we had hoped for. I have been in a number of churches, in different parts of the State, since the Congress and the boys in all cases are still talking about "The Texan". It is an understatement to say your presentation was well received, because it was great! Most of all though, was the way you brought the real life truth and spiritual emphasis into each part of your performance. It is really exciting to see how God works through your presentation.

If we, of the Louisiana Baptist Men and Boys Department, can be of any help to you in the future, please feel free to call on us. If anyone desires a recommendation for your presentation as "The Texan", Christian group or other, please have them contact us or use this correspondence to convey our enthusiasm for your work.

Sincerely,

Cal Jones
Associate Director
Baptist Men & Boys

CJ/bm

Robert L. Lee, Executive Director   Box 311, Alexandria, Louisiana 71301   Area (318) 443-3611

Letter from the Louisiana Baptist Convention

ROBERT COX

ILLINOIS BAPTIST STATE ASSOCIATION

Assisting in establishing and developing Baptist churches

LAY MOBILIZATION DEPARTMENT
BOB STUCKEY, DIRECTOR   217/786-2630

JIM WOOTTON, MISSIONARY-IN-RESIDENCE

January 25, 1980

Mr. Robert Cox, THE TEXAN
330 Robin Hill Lane
Duncanville, Texas 75137

Dear Robert:

It has been two months since you shared at the Illinois Royal Ambassador Congress. Many responses from men and boys alike have been received, all of which were very complmentary. Some of the comments are: "The Texan was really great." " I tried not to blink my eyes for fear I would miss somthing!" "Not only was The Texan great with his gun handling, but his Christian testimony was outstanding and a challenge to me." "I really liked The Texan. He was fantastic."

Yes, Robert, your program was excellent. I really appreciated the evidence of your commitment to Christ, both through your testimony as well as by your presentations. Your skill in gun handling and sharing proper rules for using a gun were outstanding.

I recommend your presentation without reservation and know that it would be a delightful presentation as well as a challenge to live so as to bring honor and glory to Jesus Christ, our Lord and Savior.

Again, thank you for sharing with us here in Illinois.

In His service,

James L. Wootton

James L. Wootton

Box 3486, Springfield, Illinois 62708 / (217) 786-2600 / James H. Smith, Executive Secretary

Letter from the Illinois Baptist State University

IF ONLY I COULD READ

With my trucking job, I found that dealing with trying to read the bills of lading and street signs began to wear on me. This was especially true when my dispatcher would call me on the radio and give me a street name and address to pick up freight. I would attempt to spell the street name by sounding out what I thought I heard. Needless to say, it was not always correct. At those times my dispatcher would call me and ask, "What's taking so long?"

I sure didn't want to tell him that I couldn't spell the name of the street and had no one to help me. I had to get some help.

A big turning point came when I heard about the book Mapsco. It had the names of the streets and the corresponding map. I would look at the spelling of the street on the bill of lading and match it up with the name of the street in the back of the Mapsco. This was a huge blessing for me, relieving so much of my stress.

Me driving for East Texas Motor Freight

In 1980, I had another opportunity to audition for a movie being shot in Dallas. The movie was Ruby and Oswald, starring Michael Lerner and Frederic Forrest. The film was about the assassination of President Kennedy. I was blessed get a part as a detective. Miracle of miracles, there was no script to read. I was playing a detective who put Oswald in the squad car at the Texas Theatre in Oak Cliff, where Oswald was arrested. I drove the actor playing Oswald to the police station.

A side note to this scene is that the detective, James R. Leavelle, played his own part in the movie. In fact, he was handcuffed to Oswald after Kennedy's assassination, in the famous newspaper photo when Ruby shot Oswald.

In 1981, while performing at a shopping mall in Abilene Texas, a man watching the show approached me and asked if I would come to Dallas and perform my show in one of the hotels for a private fundraising party. I told him I would be glad to and that, because I lived in Dallas, I would not need to be reimbursed for travel expenses. From that show in Dallas, I received several more contracts to do shows for other parties, conventions, and other events. It really boosted my ego to have people tell me that they wanted me to perform.

In 1982, I was in Chicago performing at a convention for a few days. When I returned to Dallas and went to work on Monday morning, I was told that East Texas Motor Freight Line had been sold to Arkansas Best Freight Line

(ABF). ETMF had close to 200 employees in Dallas. Unfortunately, ABF did not want to take any of them. In the past, when union freight lines would merge, they would dovetail all employees according to seniority. Most of the time there would be more employees than needed, and the lowest seniority employees would be released.

    I guess through negotiations with the union, ABF agreed take 50 of us drivers and dockworkers. I was number 47 on that list. With 23 years of employment, I felt so grateful to keep my job. ABF employees with one year of seniority kept their job, and hundreds of ETMF employees who had 22 years of seniority were let go.

    The owner of ETMF Systems was Bum Bright, who also owned the Dallas Cowboys Football Team. I guess letting so many ETMF employees lose their jobs was a better business deal for him. After a short term of working for ABF, I could tell they were trying to find ways to get rid of the former ETMF employees. After investing so many years in the industry, I was looking forward to retirement. I did not want to jeopardize my job by taking off work to travel for shows, commercials, and motion picture work. I called Joy, my booking agent, and told her that, because of my current work situation, I would no longer be available for auditions or for gun shows.

It was a difficult decision, but I knew it was best for my family.

After about six years with ABF and not doing entertainment work, I once again decided to try to find help for my reading problem. Although I'd run into so many brick walls in the past, I thought to myself, "Maybe things have changed. Maybe there's someone out there who can help me this time."

So, in 1988, I signed up for community college again. They placed me in a learning skills center, which was a large classroom for students with various problems. We all needed help, some for Math, English, Science or reading. They assigned me to a male instructor who handed me a book and told me to start reading. He told me to use the dictionary to look up any words I didn't understand. He said this would help me learn how to break down the word. I found myself staring at the dictionary most of the time. I had no idea what the symbols around the words meant. I tried two different nights and was got nowhere. I spoke to the instructor and told him this was not working for me.

His response was, "Let's try something different."

He took me over to a computer that had some kind of a program he thought might help me. I spent that evening on the computer, and two nights later I returned for another class and continued working on that program. When I finished, I went back to the instructor and told him I was finished.

Rather than let me quit, he gave me another task on the computer. I returned to the computer and started trying to get the program started, and I could not do It. I found the instructor and told him I was having trouble getting the program started. He came over to the desk and tried also. He too was having trouble and could not get the program started. He became frustrated, took the instruction book, flopped it on the desk, and abruptly said to me, "Just read the instructions, and it will tell you what to do." And then he walked off.

IF ONLY I COULD READ

I sat there looking at the computer and the instruction book thinking to myself, "If I could read this damn thing, I would not be in this class."

This was unbelievable. I started laughing hysterically, so loud that I was disrupting the entire class. I didn't give a damn. I walked out laughing so hard that by the time I got to my car, my laughter had turned to tears. All I could think was, "How much longer am I going to continue to waste my time on something so impossible." I just wanted to fight or hurt somebody. I truly did not know what to do with my feelings. I was so irrational that I drove down to a lake about a mile and a half from the college. I truly wanted to start a fight with somebody.

There was a small park where I stopped, got out of the car, and walked around, telling myself just how dumb and stupid I was. I wanted to hit something, so I kicked my tire hard, so hard that I thought I broke my ankle. It hurt so bad, but it got rid of my anger. As I stood there leaning against my car with my ankle throbbing, I did a lot of thinking.

If I am so dumb and stupid, how can I draw, design, build furniture, select music for my gun show, put a 30-minute act together, and teach myself how to twirl guns to music. Can dummies do these things? My life was making no sense to me. Something was not right, and I didn't understand.

In 1980, the Jerry Lewis Muscular Dystrophy Telethon was filmed at the Dallas Convention Center. I do not remember how this happened, but I was scheduled to be on this nationally produced show, and I was so excited. When they told me I needed to get ready to go onstage, I got so nervous. They'd come to me and say that they were going to hold me off a bit, because they were going to run the Dallas Cowboy Cheerleaders on stage first. That was a bit of a letdown, knowing I had to wait. Then after a bit, they came back and told me to get ready to go on, and I would get all psyched up again.

Wouldn't you know it, they came to me again and said they were going to hold me back and let some singer go ahead of me. This was really starting to get disappointing.

Here they came again. "Get ready Robert, you'll be going out soon."

They'd get me started and then bring out the Dallas Cowboy Cheerleaders again. I was beginning to think they were not going to let me perform.

When I arrived at the convention center that day, I had given my music to the sound technicians and told them the tape was all set to start playing. All that they had to do, at that point, was start it. Finally, I got to go out on stage. When it came time to twirl my guns, I waited for the music to the start, and it did not, so I kept standing there, waiting and not knowing what was happening. I knew that I had to do something, so I started twirling my guns. Halfway through the routine, the music suddenly blasted. This really messed me up, and I felt like a fool, hardly professional. I had told some friends of mine that I was going to be on the Jerry Lewis Telethon and to watch for me. I wish I had not told them that. What an experience.

CHAPTER 10

Sometime in 1983, I heard of another class to help people with reading problems. It was sponsored by a group called Operation Lift. Despite all I'd been through, I was hopeful they could figure out my problem. I contacted them to find where and when they would hold their classes. I showed up at the appointed time thinking, "Let's try it one more time. Maybe something will be new and different."

When I walked into the room, all of the students were teenagers. I was the only adult, except for the two young female instructors. I felt embarrassed to be the only older person who needed help with reading. But I didn't walk out. I told them I was there to get help with my reading problem. They said the first thing I needed to do was take a test, which was to write my ABC's, so I did. Then one of the young instructors told me that she was sorry they could not help me because I knew my ABC's. I was at the end of my rope. I became very emotional and angry, because none of this made

IF ONLY I COULD READ

sense. I knew that I was scaring the young girls. There I was, this big, angry, frustrated, and crying old man.

One of the young ladies told me she would get in touch with the lady in charge of the program. She said she'd tell her about me, and she would possibly call me. A few days later I did receive a call from a Mrs. Cox, who told me the young girl had told her about my problem. She suggested that I come over to her house and tell her about my difficulties. A few nights later, I arrived at her house, and she handed me a book and asked me to read to her.

After a few minutes, she stopped me and said, "This is your problem: You are dyslexic."

Of course, I had no idea what dyslexia was, so she gave me brief explanation that I did not understand. Mrs. Cox suggested that I go to Richland Community College and see a lady name Jean Brewer, who was in charge of a reading class that taught phonics. Of course, I had not heard of phonics.

I called Mrs. Brewer and got an appointment to meet with her one afternoon after work. She explained to me what dyslexia was; that it was an umbrella term that covered several learning disabilities. She gave me an example by reading a letter that a person with dyslexia had written. She could tell just by reading the letter that a person was dyslexic. This was amazing to me. She told me about several famous people in history who were dyslexic.

What a tremendous relief! I cried all the way home, praising God, saying, "Thank you God I'm dyslexic. I thought I was stupid."

After all these years, finally there's hope. "Thank God I'm dyslexic!"

I was waving my arms and crying, while driving on LBJ Freeway in rush hour traffic. I could see the people in other vehicles look at me like I was drunk or crazy.

I didn't care what they thought of me. I was just so relieved.

Mrs. Brewer suggested I sign up for their class that would be starting in a week or so, so I did. The first night of class I was very nervous about what it would be like and the people that would be in this class. There were about 10 to 12 other people in the class, all adults like me. I was very surprised there were other people with problems like mine. For the first time, after all of those years of trying to get help, I truly felt encouraged, like this was going to work. Because the class started at 6:00 pm, I knew I'd have trouble getting off work in time to get there.

 I thought long and hard for a few days, trying to figure out how I was going to be able to pull this off. I approached my terminal manager, Marvin Miller, who was the ultimate boss at my workplace, and told him that I needed his help. It was difficult to tell my story to someone at my workplace, but I knew I had to do it. I told Mr. Miller I had a problem with reading, and if I could improve my reading, I would be a more efficient employee.

 I explained that quite often I would have to write on the bills of lading that freight was damaged. I told him that if my reading improved, so would my spelling, and I would be able to write more precise notations. My proposal was, if they would let me off 30 minutes early for two days weekly, I'd be willing to give up two 15-minute breaks that I was entitled to each day. I also agreed to not take my normal lunch break. On those days, I'd end up giving him an extra hour of productive time.

 He told me that, while he didn't know anything about dyslexia, he was willing to help anyone that was trying to help themselves. I hoped that I had made an offer he could not refuse, and he didn't. That relieved a lot of stress in my life.

In the class I began taking, we all had the same problem, so when we would mess up or make mistakes, we could laugh with each other and not feel embarrassed or stupid. That made it fun and easier to learn. I took two semesters at Richland College. I have a book that I purchased, and at the age of 50 years old, I read my very first book. The title of the book is, "Getting the Love You Want," by Harville Hendryx, PhD. The title is a little misleading. It's a guide for couples on how to better communicate with each other. That was 30 years ago, and today that book sits in my office on the shelf. I was so thrilled to be able to read, and although my reading skills are not perfect, I can now read whatever I choose.

In 1990 Joy, my agent, called about an audition for a one-time call for the Lucite Paint Company. I think the casting director had seen me, or I had worked with him some years before. He asked me for an audition, but I really wasn't thrilled because it would require me to take off two or three days to shoot a commercial. If my employer happened to know that I was taking off to shoot a commercial, I could lose my job.

I did go to the audition, and they told me they would be shooting the commercial in a few days, and that they would let me know in a couple of days if I got the part. Three or four days went by, and never heard a word. I assumed I did not get a part. I felt relieved, even though I would've loved to shoot the commercial.

A few days later at work, I hurt my back and the company sent me to their doctor. The doctor said I had pulled muscles in my back, and I needed to recover by not working for two weeks. I went back to the office and told my employer what the doctor had said. I left work and drove home. When I walked in the front door, my phone was ringing, and it was my agent, Joy.

She said, "Robert you got the part."

I was surprised, because I thought that they would have already shot the commercial by now. Talk about perfect timing. Now that I could not work for two weeks, I was free to shoot the commercial.

It took two days to shoot. While we were shooting the commercial, the director would give me instructions of where to walk and stand, and I was sure that I was doing exactly what he asked. He kept telling me to do it again, turn my head, and look up a certain way. I felt certain that I was doing exactly as he instructed, but somehow something was going wrong. I could tell the director was getting annoyed with me. I must admit that I was frustrated with him too. For some reason, I was having a rough time following his instructions.

But in the end, we finished the commercial, and I was proud of my work. The ad ran for two years as a national commercial. I felt so blessed, because this one paid well.

Sometime in 1989, my wife read an article in the Dallas Morning News about an Adult Dyslexia Support

Group. She thought I should look into it. Maybe I could get some help and understanding there. I went to one of the meetings, and naturally everyone was dyslexic except for the two ladies who were leading the group. It was a relief to be in another group of like-minded people. Almost everyone told me what their life had been like, and I realized we all have had similar experiences. So much of the time our parents or our teachers told us, "If you would only try harder, you could do it." If trying harder would have worked, we would have been reading better by now. We all felt like the teachers had the same expectations for us as they did for the students who did not have reading problems.

We had guest speakers that put on a program for us. Along with the speakers, others in the group would share their life experiences. So many of our members talked about being placed into a class with other disabled students. I cannot imagine going through that experience. There is no such thing as a "one size fits all" disability.

After a few months in this group, I became the facilitator. One of my duties was to find guest speakers. After a while, I was asked to speak to different groups and at various conferences. After telling my story numerous times, the #1 question that came up was, "How in the hell did you keep your job?"

The truth is, I had developed street smarts. I realized God blessed me with adaptability. Over time, I learned that I couldn't afford to be shy in seeking help.

We ran ads in the local papers about our Dyslexia Support Group. I always included my phone number as a contact. It was amazing how many phone calls I would get from people who wanted help for themselves, a coworker, or a loved one. As facilitator, I was invited to serve on the board of directors for the local National Orton Dyslexic Society.

I was given a brochure, published by another organization that cited some alarming statistics about people who cannot read. I came across a shocking statistic, that 91% of all prison inmates have a severe reading problem or cannot read it all. The more I thought about it, the more sense this made. Look at all the trouble I got into in order to avoid reading. I was so very fortunate that I was able to get a good-paying job through my parents. If I had to fill out job applications, it would have been a disaster, because I could not read the questions.

IF ONLY I COULD READ

I consider myself an honest person. However, if I was hungry and didn't have a job, and no money, I don't know what I would have done.

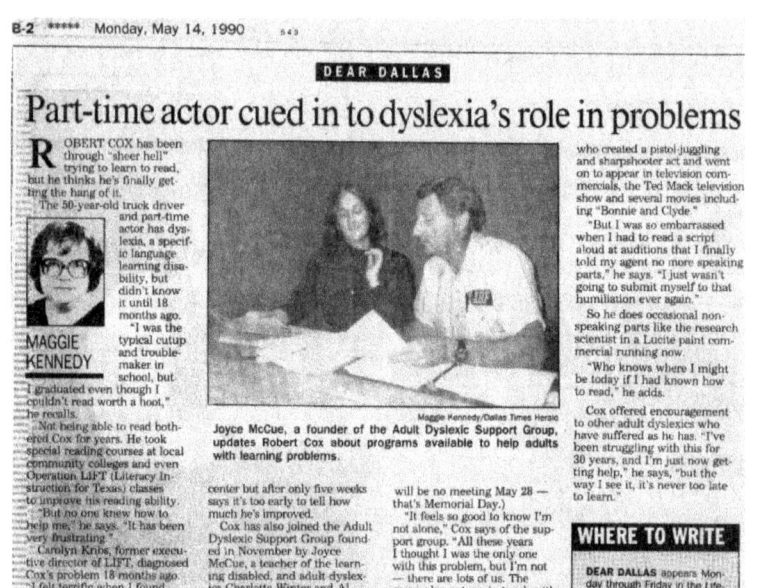

Article from Dear Dallas

REFLECTIONS

When I look back over the last 80 years of my life, I realize how embarrassed and humiliated I had felt about my reading problem. I often cried out to God for help and thought He didn't hear me. Now I know that He was there all the time, helping and guiding me. He protected me from remembering the details of the tragic shooting accident. He also made it possible for me to earn a living as a truck driver, as an actor, and as a performer.

I believe that God shaped me, like I was shaping the working parts of my guns, filing and then polishing each part as needed. Then I'd place the parts back into the gun, return it to the holster, and draw. I'd continue this process until I knew that it worked well for me. God guided my life with the same love and compassion.

I strongly believe that God has a Divine purpose for each of us, and that He uses difficulties and hardships to build our character. He molds and shapes us to serve Him. My biggest fear is that I have missed His purpose for my life. I know that I will continue to live in a way that seems pleasing to Him.

A few years ago, while I was reading my Bible, a particular verse stood out and has helped me cope with my past. I knew that I trusted the Lord and believed that he was guarding me. Proverbs 20: 24 states, "Since the Lord is directing my steps why try to understand everything that happens along the way." This verse has given me such peace of mind regarding my past, future, and what I considered problems. I now realize that He was indeed preparing me for something for Him.

Thinking back to the terrible accident where I, as a young boy, fired the shot that killed the little boy, I knew that I wanted to do whatever I could to prevent this from happening again.

My wife and I had two sons, so we started teaching them about guns. I bought them their first guns at ages 10 and 12, and I was adamant about teaching them that guns are dangerous and need to be respected. So, I taught them how to shoot and clean, to store them, and to be responsible, as well as never touching a gun without an adult present. I also told them to never tell their friends that there were guns in the house. My greatest fear was that my experience would be repeated.

Now we have six grandsons and one great grandson. On each of their fifth birthdays, I buy them their first gun, a small 30" or 32" 22 single shot rifle. The gun's name is a Chipmunk. I engrave their names on the stock and the date that they received it from Grandpa Robert. Each of their guns match their father's.

As you can tell, I believe in teaching them young. With their fathers' help, I teach them how to shoot, clean and respect the danger of a gun. I pray that this effort will prevent them having a tragedy like mine.

I have had hopes and dreams, like everyone does, about things I have wanted to do in my life, in spite of my reading and dyslexia problem. I have, with God's help, been able to accomplish to a certain extent every dream that I've ever had.

Considering all I have written, the last thing I would like to share with you may not seem like a big deal. But for me, it is a very big deal. I remember all of the birthdays and special occasions I've experienced throughout my life. Not being able to read, my wife would have to read my birthday cards aloud at my parties. No one ever asked why I didn't read them myself, but I always felt awkward because I could not.

I remember the first card I was able to read aloud, all by myself. It was given to me be my wife on our anniversary. The love I have for her and the beautiful words in the card brought me to tears as I read it.

Like I said, reading an anniversary card is no big deal to most people. But when you've lived your whole life not being able to read, it's a wonderful experience.

Looking back on everything, all of the things that made me the man I am today, I have to say I've had a great life.

EPILOGUE

I retired from the freight line industry on June 27, 1992, with a total of 35 years of service. I had earned a sterling silver belt buckle award for driving one million miles in the city of Dallas, all without a chargeable accident. My father, stepmother, and I, together had 102 years of service in the trucking industry. My father had 27 years, my stepmother had 40 years, and I had 35 years.

After retiring in 1992, I went to work part time setting up trade shows. I now have 27 years in that industry.

At age 80, I continue to work. I believe that work is extremely healthy, both for the mind and for the body.

I've been thinking about my generation's work ethics, versus the current generation. It seems that we started working at a much earlier age, and we truly valued our jobs.

IF ONLY I COULD READ

I started working at the age of 10. The following is a list of the various jobs that I've had.

Age 10, Pin boy at a bowling alley.

Age 11, 7-11 Store keeping coolers stocked and running the cash register.

Age 11-12, Stock boy, soda jerk, and clerk at a large chain drug store. One night a "customer" approached me with a receipt in his hand, as if he had paid for something. He asked if I could help load a TV set that he had purchased into his truck. I assumed the receipt was for this TV. The next day I found out that no one had sold the TV; the man had stolen it. I guess, you might say, that made me an accomplice.

From age 11-12, I also worked at a grocery store, sacking groceries for customers. Like most kids, I mowed yards at this age.

During my senior year in high school, I sold newspapers door-to-door. This was to support my wife and myself.

Throughout my life, I've maintained employment in the following industries:

Valet parking for private parties

Chauffeuring

Security at private parties

Sold vacuum cleaners by appointment

Entertainer (Gun shows, commercials, and acting)

Truck driving

Retail popcorn store owner

Sold long distance telephone service

Sold home security systems

Photographer for a magazine (which involved flying in military aircraft, photographing military balls, and Mrs. Senior Texas Pageants)

Set up trade shows for Decorators Union

Air courier for the Treasury Department

Oh, and in case you were wondering, I did eventually get revenge on the kid who tricked me into eating Ex-Lax when I was in grade school. It took a few decades, but I finally got Ricky back. The opportunity came when my wife and I opened a retail popcorn store. We sold circus popcorn and ice cream. Some of the ice cream came with different types of candy sprinkled on top.

One day I went to the local drugstore and bought a package of chocolate Ex-Lax. I ground it up and put it in a container. I put a big X on the top of the container and told my employees not to use it, and then I waited.

One day Ricky and his wife came in, and I told him I wanted him to try a new flavor of ice cream. I mixed up the ice cream with all of the Ex-Lax. I gave it to him, and he took a couple of bites.

He told me, "That's good Robert," and then he gave some to his wife.

I became very worried, because I did not want her to eat any of that ice cream.

Later in the afternoon, I thought I would hear from Ricky, but I never did. When we closed the shop that day, we went by his house to see what had happened. So far, Ricky hadn't noticed anything. At that point, I could not contain myself. I told him what I had done, and then I went home. About 6:30 the next morning, I received a call from Ricky.

He said, "Robert, it hit me about midnight. Don't you think that 36 years is a very long time to carry a grudge?"

I figured he was probably right, but I finally got him!

Funny thing, he no longer goes around laughing and telling the story of what he did to me in the fifth grade.

ROBERT COX

ABOUT THE AUTHOR

Robert Cox is a native of Dallas, Texas. He worked as a truck driver for 35 years, before retiring in 1992. Robert has travelled the country, working as a part-time actor. After mastering the "quick draw" skill at a young age, he mesmerized crowds at gun shows, performing as "The Texan." He currently resides in Dallas with Patricia Cox, his wife of 19 years. He has 5 sons, 9 grandchildren and 2 great grandchildren. *If Only I Could Read* is his first book.